Heart

Supporting Fellow Sufferers of Benign Arrhythmia

You Are Not Alone

Jen Penrose

Copyright © 2018 Jen Penrose

Front cover illustration by Frank W Smith
Author of Wolf Song
https://www.amazon.com/Frank-W-Smith/e/B009OCFNY8/ref=dp_byline_cont_ebooks_1

Disclaimer

This book is aimed at those who have had the relevant tests in relation to their arrhythmia and have been diagnosed as having a benign condition.

Any mention of alternative potions and notions that I, and others have found helpful, are for reference purposes only. I would urge you to check with your own medical practitioners before trying them for yourself.

Links to online forums and groups are not verified by me, with the exception of those linking to known medical practitioners. Some have been helpful to me and I have no qualms in saying that two in particular (2 & 3) saved my sanity. There will be a list of links to relevant sites at the end of the book.

Any mention of my own theories or those put forward by others, will have come from experience and therefore, from a layman view point. I am not promoting my suggestions as universal truths, rather they are a presentation of my experiences, my research and my interaction with the many sufferers I am in contact with. I hope that some of the ideas and experiences resonate with the reader.

I have been granted permission to publish stories shared with me by others, including some posts from our Facebook Group. (1)

I am a retired counselling therapist and supervisor. I began working in the helping professions in 1991, and in private practice from 1996, until my retirement in 2016. I was a senior BACP accredited therapist and I retired earlier than expected due to this condition. This was because I felt it would have been unethical to continue. Whilst some of my thoughts and ideas come from my many years in practice, what I write is mainly from my personal philosophies about illness, life and disposition. I hope that I encourage you to undertake your own personal research into your condition, and its possible causes. This book is food for thought; a kicking off of ideas that may lead you to your own, unique, healing path.

If anything I write is unclear, feel free to join our Facebook group where I, or others might be able to explain further. (1)

LIST OF CONTENTS

Introduction

Thank You

Why Palps – Why Me?

The Vagus Nerve

Roemheld Syndrome

The Loss of Self

Loss of Trust in The Process of Life

Facebook Group Feedback

Emily's Story

Kathy's Story

L. MacDiarmid's Story

H.R's Story

G.S's Story

Jen's Story

Addendum

Conclusion

Links and References

Introduction

This book has been writing itself for many years. It has been difficult to get it on to paper because the story is ever evolving, as are my own heartbeat issues, which at the point of writing, have been with me for 10 years.

I am curious by nature and this inquisitiveness has enabled me to think about my own condition in more depth, rather than a non-questioning acceptance of it. I understand that although benign PVC's (Premature ventricular contractions – or extra beats that begin in the heart's lower chambers – the ventricles), and PAC's (premature atrial contractions – being in the upper chambers of the heart – the atria) are deemed physically harmless, on a psychological level I believe in most cases they impair quality of life. It might depend on the severity and type of arrhythmia, and how it impacts lives and ways of being. For me and many others, our lives are minimised and edited by our disobedient hearts.

There are many people who manage their arrhythmia very well and will perhaps argue that we do need to ignore the whacky beats and get on with living our lives. I am open to this criticism and applaud those of you who have developed a way to live your lives unperturbed. This book is devoted to those lives that are ruled by their arrhythmia, and to those people who, like myself, suffer from couplets, bigeminy and trigeminy, SVT and Afib, chest pain, syncope or near syncope, and many other symptoms that appear to be part of the same problem.

You will read in 'my story' how, in desperation, I trawled the internet looking for answers. The first place I visited was a website called 'No More Panic' (2), founded by a woman called Nicola Pinney. The site has a forum with various sections, one section is named: 'Symptoms' and is the place where I found many fellow sufferers who were looking for answers. Some had found their own particular cure or ways to manage symptoms. It was there that I came to believe that these whacky heart rhythms were a symptom, rather than an illness in their own right – but a symptom of what? Trying to find the answer to that question has been a difficult journey. If you have chosen to read this book, it is very likely that you are on this same, somewhat lonely and isolating trip too.

During my time on the forum of 'No More Panic,' I found I was able to manage a little better. This was not because things had improved, but because I had found other sufferers who could empathise on an experiential level. It wasn't easy for friends and family to deal with a woman with anxiety and fear crowding out her days; a woman who hung on to walls as she walked, one that no longer socialised, who no longer smiled or laughed.

One day, sometime during 2009, while visiting the NMP forum, I noted that a retired doctor had answered a few of our questions. He had his own forum (3) and visited NMP every now and then to try and help us. His name was Rutheford Rane, MD, a retired neurologist in America.

When I visited his forum, I found many more people who were just as confused and frightened as me. Interacting with fellow suffers and reading Dr Rane's answers to our questions, made the world of difference to my previous sense of isolation.

Sadly, in mid-2013 Dr Rane, or RLR as he was fondly known by members of his forum, stopped replying to questions. It wasn't unusual for him to be absent throughout April time, because he helped with a charity for children during that period. By mid-June he had still not appeared and knowing how dedicated he was to his forum and to us, the members recognised that it was very possible that our dear RLR had passed away. He was after all 90 years old. Those who had provided the forum for RLR (Chemical Forums) have kindly reinstated it for read only purposes. The information you will find on the forum, I believe, is invaluable and worth exploring.

Dr. Rane was not keen on members of his forum using it for socialising, and so with his permission, in 2010, I opened a Facebook group and Dr. Rane allowed me to place a link to it on his forum. We moved the Facebook group once in 2011 due to privacy issues at the time. The second one (1) is still running and at the point of writing, has seven thousand members with many new people joining each day.

Facebook Group members share their experiences with other members. With their permission, I have included a few posts from the group in this book.

Most of the feedback is about loss, about distress and about lack of joy. There are some who are less impacted by the condition and are able to lead fulfilling lives. I am not sure if this is about severity, disposition, strength and how much support people have. Perhaps all of those, or none. From my own experience, I had years with only atrial ectopic beats and just a few PVC's here and there. I learned to manage those. However, as time went on, they evolved, giving me small bouts of Afib and SVT throughout the day, along with pre-syncope. Never knowing when these symptoms will appear, makes planning outings, even a bus ride, very difficult.

I have been gifted with stories from Kathy, H.R, L. MacDiarmid, Emily and GS. They have given me permission to include them in this book. These stories expose the devastating impact this condition has on lives. They highlight the need for research and more empathy for our distress. We need our unheard cries for help and the losses we suffer, recognised and supported.

I have been told by a variety of people that they are harmless and I should just get on with it. I think that getting on with it is to accept something as a given, therefore rendering things out of our control. There is a sense of defeat in that for me personally, as though there is not, nor will there ever be a cure. I know that to find a cure, or full management, more research would need to be done.

I am not a medical practitioner and that does limit my understanding of how cure can be achieved. I simply hope to set medical minds thinking by bringing all our voices to the table, and I hope that this book is the beginning of a new understanding.

Thank You

My thanks to all the admins of our Facebook group who helped admin the group from the outset: Georgina, Will, Louise and Emma. Much thanks to all the other admins from all over the globe who have given their time ever since: Maryellen, Frank, Helana, Alisha, Jo, Kathy and Vince. I continue as founder member and an admin; however, Vince is at this time, the main admin for the group.

Thank you to all the wonderful members who have added to our knowledge and who support each other on a daily basis.

Roemheld Syndrome

Why Palps – Why Me?

"Sickness is not sent by the gods or taken away by them. It has a natural basis. If we can find the cause, we can find the cure."

Hippocrates

I want to refer to PAC's and PVC's as palpitations or palps, because it is a term used by members of the heart palpitation Facebook group (1). Please do not be fooled by the terms 'palpitations' or 'palps' – these are not referring to the type of pounding in the heart that one feels when running. What most experience is a skipping, jumping, fluttering, pausing, thumping, angry heart that people are dealing with on a daily basis – sometimes every moment of every day.

It is my belief that I have a condition called Roemheld Syndrome. While I am not proposing this as a cause for everyone, it is worth reading up on and deciding for yourself if RS could apply to you. Before I go into more detail about Roemheld Syndrome, it is important that I list other possible causes for your heart palps. These have come to my attention via forums and the Facebook group and therefore, I have not investigated or researched them in full. However, they come up regularly and need a mention:

Prescribed and OTC Medications:

I do not have an extensive list of medications that mention heart rhythm difficulties as a potential side effect. Often when arrhythmia is listed, it appears under the uncommon or rare side effect section. It is best to read the leaflet that comes with your meds just to see if heart arrhythmia is stated as a possible side effect. It is good to remember that people appear to metabolize medications differently, just as they do food. In this case, just because it might list arrhythmia as a side effect, may not mean this is the cause for you. For example, some people who take SSRI antidepressants report heart rhythm issues, whereas others find taking them relieves their palps. People on thyroxine often report palpitations, others find that taking it is a solution. Whether this is the disease or the medication, I am unsure. It is always worth a mention to your doctor, just to see if further exploration might help. Some people who have stomach issues and are prescribed medications to reduce stomach acid find great relief from gastritis and GERD. Some however, find these medications make them feel worse or have side effects that outweigh any help they may gain. This brings us back to the idea of cause, rather than symptoms. Ask yourself if the symptoms began after starting a particular medication. If you think it is possible, talk with your doctor who may help test the idea out with you.

Over the counter medications, especially decongestants, are notorious for causing racing heart and palpitations, even for those who do not normally suffer. Some OTC pain relief meds contain caffeine and, in my opinion, caffeine is best avoided. Again, it is essential to educate yourself on the side effects of anything you ingest. If possible, avoid stimulants altogether and switch to decaffeinated teas and coffee. Dark chocolate, too much sugar, sweeteners

Chocolate : CACAO Nibs have caffeine?

especially aspartame have been reported as culprits by some people, including me. It is best to test out anything you feel suspicious about. I found it interesting that some people found their toothpaste caused them issues. However, not wanting to create paranoia, my message is that of a process of elimination.

Hormones:

Many female members join our group during pregnancy and continue to suffer some time after the birth. Pre- menopause and menopause are reported by many of our members as being the cause of their heart palpitations. It is interesting that some females only experience them during certain days of their cycle. Others report palpitations when on hormonal birth control. I have read that during pregnancy cardiac output increases and is put forward as a possible cause. Others think about the fluctuation of hormones. Some, like myself, wonder if the fluctuation that might occur could possibly have an impact on other hormones. After all, hormones are chemical messengers and important for somatic equilibrium. Different hormones have different roles – for example, adrenaline prepares the body for fight or flight. If the endocrine system becomes out of balance or disturbed, is it possible that this would have an effect on the efficiency of the whole messaging system?

Adrenaline:
↳ lack of sleep ?

Quite a few members of the Facebook Group have reported palpitations with progesterone implants and birth control coils. It is worth discussing things with your doctor who may be willing to look into this with you?

During my searches I came across quite a bit of information about EDC's (Endocrine Disrupting Chemicals). These are "a broad category of compounds used in consumer products, electronics and agriculture, have been associated with a diverse array of health issues.

These non-natural chemicals or mixtures of chemicals can mimic, block, or interfere with the way the body's hormones work. They have been linked to human health issues related to sperm quality, fertility, abnormalities in sex organs, endometriosis, early puberty, nervous system function, immune function, cancers, breathing problems, metabolic issues, obesity, heart health, growth, neurological and learning disabilities, and more.

Exposure to EDCs can happen anywhere and come from the air we breathe, the food we eat, and the water we drink. EDCs can also enter the body through the skin and by transfer from mother to foetus (across the placenta) or mother to infant (via breast feeding) if a woman has EDCs in her body." The Hormone Health Network (4)

I thought EDC's was worth a mention because you may want to read the article for yourself and look for more information if this interests you. There are many articles and papers on the subject to review and I hope to research further into this at some point.

A very good place to learn about hormones and how they work, is the BBC's GCSE Bitesize subjects: (5)

Just a word on an idea I have been playing with. Although fluctuating hormones might be causing palpitations during pregnancy, it is also worth reading the section on Roemheld's Syndrome and its connection with the movement of the diaphragm.

Anxiety and Depression:

Stress / Anx

Anxiety & Stress over a long time

Some people will have suffered severe stress, generalised anxiety, PTSD, depression, phobias and other disabling mental health conditions before the onset of palps. It is my belief that having anxiety or stress over a long period of time can mean that our messaging system continues to inform our sympathetic nervous system that we are living on the edge and need to be ready to run or fight, even when we do not. This overworking takes its toll, causing the system to become confused, irritated, and inappropriately activated. Some might simplify this by saying the nervous system has developed bad habits.

yes

Many people who suffer from anxiety and/or long-term stress often report physical symptoms which they, and sometimes their doctors, do not marry up to any mental anguish. There are all sorts of ideas around the physical symptoms of mental distress. Producing a seminar on the subject 23 years ago, allowed me to think about the mind/body connection in detail. My conclusion proposed a total view, incorporating genes, environment, social disposition and defence mechanisms. Since then the world has moved forward with alternative thinking and therapy being more mainstream. People are aware of healthy eating, exercise and the effects of stress. There is an openness about feelings being the centre of illness. However, much of the hype comes from those wanting to make money from other people's weaknesses. That is not to say that good nutrition, exercise and relaxation are not helpful; on the contrary I promote the idea of finding ways to nourish your body to enable it to heal and flourish. But if doing so impacts on your budget or your anxiety levels, by putting yourself under pressure to work hard at healing, the object is defeated.

Living with anxiety can be disabling. My years as a therapist allowed me to witness crippling attacks. One agency I worked for had a stock of paper bags so that we could give them to people during a panic/anxiety attack. They would breath in and out of the bag until they felt calmer. This does work in the short term, but it does not tackle the problem. Since suffering from intermittent anxiety brought about by storms of palps, I use this method when I have paper bags available. I would suggest that you do not use this method without checking with your doctor as it may be unadvisable with certain conditions.

Panic-attacks.co.uk, explain how this technique helps with hyperventilation because it "will cause you to re-inhale the carbon dioxide that you exhaled." This technique is just one of many they list to help you with panic and I would encourage people to stop off and read the site and its free course (6).

It would be easy for me to write more about anxiety here – however, I am afraid I may go off the intended subject. I will say that I believe most often, but not always, anxiety is rooted in something far deeper. This deeper meaning, which manifests as anxiety is less accessible and does require some sort of intervention. However, the type of anxiety most of us experience in response to our palps is very here and now; an unbidden reflex.

Mini Panic Attack

As most of us know, we are kept alive by a perfectly working nervous system. We do not have to think our hearts to beat, we can leave that all to the unconscious workings of our internal systems. Can't we? We now understand that thoughts and fears not only impact our minds but can also create somatic responses. Just by thinking about something scary can set off a mini panic attack, even those not prone to them. For example, watching horror movies, being a passenger in a speeding car and so on. Many people seek out the feeling by taking scary rides at fun fairs. Temporary panic is something I assume everyone has experienced. But what happens to a system (mind and body) that is constantly bombarded with panic? It is my contention that things get thrown out of balance and the nervous system becomes oversensitive and confused. I will talk more about this is the chapter: Loss of Trust in the Process of life.

Repetitive Panic

There are many, like myself, who report that they were not suffering from anxiety before getting heart palpitations, rather, they became anxious because of them. By the time a person visits their doctor or cardiologist, very often they present as a fearful, anxious patient. This often leads to the diagnosis: benign ectopic beats, probably caused by anxiety. In this case, after all investigations are complete, it appears that there is no more to be done. You may be offered a beta blocker or other medication, but generally there is no actual cure. Perhaps you will be referred for therapy, such as CBT (Cognitive Behavioral Therapy). These therapies may help you manage things better, and if your palpitations are rooted in anxiety, they may even help you to heal. But if you are anxious because your palpitations present in quite a scary manner, no amount of CBT will make them go away, and what I believe can happen is the true cause will be missed.

I find it disappointing when people report to the group that when they present at their doctor's office with palpitations, quite often they are told the problem is anxiety. It is my belief this is a dangerous trend. An admin of our Facebook group was repeatedly told that anxiety was the cause of her symptoms by her doctor and again by her cardiologist. She had palpitations and other symptoms, for example syncope. She eventually paid to see a private cardiologist who arranged a tilt test which confirmed a condition called POTS - Postural orthostatic tachycardia syndrome. My point is: diagnosing anxiety for anything not fully understood might be easier and cheaper than it is to arrange for the relevant tests and therefore something vital could be missed. In my experience and that of others, the anxiety diagnosis is often, but not always, presented like an accusation, with a sense of blame to it, as though you should be managing your anxiety and if you are not, you are at fault. The idea that you are somehow responsible for your palpitations because you are anxious, can leave a person feeling desperate. It is that desperation I want to cover in a later chapter.

Sometimes the palpitations disappear for a while, only to return and the disappointment if that happens can be upsetting. They can be bothering you some days and not others, making them more confusing, perhaps leaving us wondering what we ate or what we did differently on bad days, compared with the good days. We can start to believe that we *are* to blame in some way for our palps. Although it is a good idea to investigate your palps, instead of doing it from guilt, e.g. *I ate some chocolate so it's my fault;* research why your body reacts to chocolate in that way.

The emotional waves that rock our equilibrium and how the self that we know can get lost in this awful turbulence that our own precious hearts cause us, is distressing. Life is never going to be the same and we know it. Perhaps when they first arrive we assume there will be a cure, I guess because humans are mostly positive creatures. We start out thinking that the right medication will put things back in order, and on occasion it will. But from my observation, once we realise these things are here to stay, either intermittently or permanently, there is a sense of loss. Many of us have had to adjust our lives and give up many things. One huge loss people refer to is the loss of joy. Many have used the words 'joy killers' and 'joy crushers' when referring to palps. I will take this sense of loss up in a later chapter, but for now, I want to stay with possible cause.

check Electrolytes

Blood Checks:

If possible, have vitamin levels checked and a a full blood count. Anaemia is known to be a cause of heart arrhythmia I am told.

If your doctor is willing, have your electrolyte levels checked. Electrolytes are in your blood, bodily fluids, and urine. These are: Calcium, chloride, magnesium, phosphate, potassium and sodium. They are found and ingested with food, drinks, and supplements. Electrolyte balance is vital for your body to function properly. It is important to stay hydrated because dehydration can lead to depletion of these minerals as can drinking too much which could flush away important minerals. WATER

If you are not allergic to coconuts, as an experiment, you could try drinking some pure coconut water for a few days, or eat a couple of bananas each day, or try other potassium rich foods and drinks such as black strap molasses which contain adequate amounts of magnesium and other electrolytes. I am amazed at the amount of people who have cured their palps this way. If you find eating foods with electrolytes helps, it might be wise to visit your doctor and report it. There could be a reason for low potassium, magnesium or even sodium levels and your doctor can order the relevant tests. For some however, no cause is identified and it could be something as simple as diet.

I was astounded to read that a few people have been relieved of palps by adding sea salt and/or Himalayan salt into their diet. People often do not intake adequate amounts of sodium in a salt free promoting society. Too much salt is not advisable either and can cause health issues. Therefore, I do not recommend this for people with high blood pressure and I most certainly advise that you discuss any supplementation with your doctor after blood tests to confirm levels. However, it is good to know that sodium is imperative for nerve and muscle function and regulation of body fluids. Sodium is involved in the body's control of blood pressure and volume. Although sodium is essential, people who consume too much sodium may have hypertension, a condition that can lead to serious illnesses such as heart disease, kidney disease, and stroke.

Foods rich in electrolytes are: banana, dates, raisins, coconut and avocado, cantaloupe and Kiwi's. Vegetable sources include spinach, beans, lentils and potato. There are many more and lists can be found all over the internet.

There is a very good site explaining electrolytes, deficiency and possible cause. (7)

Eating more magnesium rich foods can be helpful with anxiety and heart palpitations. If a supplement is required, magnesium glycinate is recommended. For more information on how magnesium can help or even abate your heart palpitations, watch Cardiologist Sanjay Gupta's You Tube on the subject.

Sanjay Gupta

A word here about Sanjay Gupta (8). He is a consultant cardiologist at York. In my experience there are few doctors or cardiologists who consider the fear, trauma and life disturbances caused by ongoing palpitations. Thanks to Dr. Rane and his forum and more recently, Sanjay Gupta, the difficulty is becoming recognised throughout the medical community.

Sanjay joined my own Facebook group in 2013, and I believe other face book groups who discuss and support the same heart issues. He took the time to read about our fears, our ups and our downs. This led him to offer us support and information. He has made a number of very helpful videos and I will leave the link to his you tube page, website and Facebook page, where he presents live videos inviting real time questions. He is also available for telephone appointments I believe. You will find details for these on his website. (8)

Acid reflux and gastroesophageal reflux disease (GERD) and Hiatus Hernia:

GERD is the main cause of my own palpitations. It is a more serious and disturbing condition than occasional acid reflux, where a few OTC medications can help. However, long term acid reflux can evolve into GERD as in my own case. This is a condition where the muscle (the sphincter) that keeps the acid inside the stomach from backing up the oesophagus, becomes loose. The inflammation from this back up of acid can cause spasms of the oesophagus, which are painful and can mimic heart attack. I know this from personal experience, and when it happens to me,

I have severe attacks of palps. The inflammation can irritate the vagus nerve (see more about the vagus in the following chapter) which in turn seems to misfire its message to the pacemaker inside the heart. It is important however to be able to distinguish between these spasms and a real heart attack. If you are unsure, please do call for medical help.

There is an operation called Nissen Fundoplication which tightens the lower oesophageal sphincter by wrapping the upper part of the stomach around the lower end of the oesophagus. However, the procedure comes with the risk of making things worse. Weighing up the risks, versus the symptoms should be discussed with your gastroenterologist. It's also often possible to research the success rates of this procedure in respect of your surgeon. I know of people who say the operation has changed their life for the better; others have been less happy.

Sometimes GERD can be subtler, especially silent reflux, which tends to happen at night or when lying flat. There are often no symptoms other than a possible hoarseness where a person feels like clearing their throat continually, also a dry cough and of course quite often, heart palpitations. Another feature of GERD can be trapped air in the oesophagus. Many people report that sometimes their palpitations will cease if they belch.

The position of the oesophagus in relation to the heart is also of importance and it is possible that when inflamed or irritated, it actually pushes against the heart and of course the heart reacts. I have been given all sorts of PPI's to try and help, however I am one of those unfortunate people who experience unbearable side effects. Many are helped by these medications and I would encourage you to try them. Ironically, a side effect is listed with some as heart rhythm disturbances. In the chapter on Roemheld's, I will discuss PPI's and their role in helping with this condition.

There are a few alternatives to try – such as DGL (deglycerised liquorice). This can act as an anti-inflammatory if taken/sucked after meals and allowed to sit in the oesophagus.

Some people find aloe to bring great relief. It is also an anti-inflammatory, which possibly treats the symptoms of inflammation in the oesophagus. Sadly, I am unable to try this due to another condition.

A flat teaspoon of sodium bicarbonate in a glass of water can neutralize stomach acid and release any pressure from gas. It is something I tend to use now and then and it does help with trapped air / gas, and therefore pressure from that on the heart.

OTC medicines which contain Sodium Bicarbonate, Sodium Alginate and Sodium Carbonate can really help because they form a barrier between the stomach and the oesophagus for up to three hours. Take this after meals and most importantly before bed. It has been so helpful to me, especially during the night.

I have come across material which promotes yogic breathing on a regular basis to heal and strengthen the sphincter – interestingly, something similar is suggested for Roemheld's, which I will discuss in the chapter on Roemhelds.

Change of diet is quite important. Eating 80% alkaline foods will cause the stomach to become less acidic and therefore less irritation will occur. There are a huge number of alkaline food lists on the net, so do research these and give it a try.

It is important to mention that it is most often assumed that too much acid is the cause – some people have too little acid, which can cause the same issues. For information on this and possible alternative treatments you can visit the website, Cure pvc's (9), which is owned by a Facebook friend, Phil.

Without wanting to repeat myself too much, I do need to stress that it is important to discuss your acid situation with your doctor. If for example you have other conditions, it is wise to check with your doctor or pharmacists to make sure that none of the above suggestions will interfere with medications or conditions.

Hiatus Hernia:

A HIATUS HERNIA is when part of your stomach moves up into your chest, most likely caused by a weakened diaphragm. There are two types of hiatus hernia:

Sliding – these are the type that move up and down, in and out of the chest area. Over 80% of hiatus hernias are sliding.

Para-oesophageal hiatus hernias – also called rolling hiatus hernias, where part of the stomach pushes up through the hole in the diaphragm next to the oesophagus. Up to 20% of hiatus hernias are Para-oesophageal.

Hiatus hernia causes the same issues as GERD. Considering the position of the HH, it is likely that it puts pressure on and can irritate the heart – which reacts with palpitations. A gastroenterologist will advise you of treatments which range from management of the symptoms, to an operation.

I have come across several people who believe that having the stomach pushed back into place by a qualified chiro-practitioner has helped. **Again, I want to stress that you seek medical advice about this.**

Injury and damage to the vagus nerve:

The vagus nerve can be damaged by diseases, for example diabetes, or by surgery to the stomach or small intestine. I know of one person whose vagus nerve was injured when her lungs were being drained. Quite a few people who have had surgery for hiatus hernia turn up on our Facebook group, complaining that since surgery they have experienced heart palpitations.

I will not pretend to have knowledge on how or why this happens. But, what I would like to share is the potential role of the vagus nerve on our palps, which became clear to me from the teachings of Dr. Rane and through my own personal research. I want to add that although I agree with Dr. Rane, because as pointed out, he did help so many of us, I do feel there is even more to the vagus nerve story than I first thought. In particular with the condition mentioned already; Roemheld Syndrome. The following chapter explores the vagus nerve.

Here is some useful, free information in relation to the management of your palps and their severity:

EFT (Emotional Freedom Tapping) – many instructional videos can be found on YouTube. My personal favourites are those by Brad Yates. I trained to perform EFT and it has helped me enormously with many physical and emotional difficulties.

Reduce or cut out fizzy drinks, coffee, tea and alcohol. Cut down on or stop eating sugar. Eat more alkaline foods. Chew food thoroughly, eat slowly and have smaller meals more often, rather than bloating, large meals. You might want to think about taking up the Fodmap way of eating, which includes cutting out gluten and lactose. Fodmap Eating is as follows:

Fermentable Oligosaccharides, Disaccharides, Monos accharides, and Polyols, which are short chain carbohydrates and sugar alcohols that are not well absorbed by the body. Although this was primarily devised for IBS, those with GERD like me, have found it helpful for this too.

Experiment with meditation and visualisation, all free for you to try.

Research acupuncture points. You can press on the heart points which incidentally, are used for anxiety.

Hand yoga / mudras. There is a specific mudra for heart palpitations which can be found in the search bar on You Tube.

Use Yogic breathing to help slow things down – I particularly like Prana Breathing. You can download a free app to help with that or once again, the practice can be found on You Tube.

Vagal manoeuvres;

Used to try and slow an episode of fast heart rate, these manoeuvres stimulate the vagus nerve. Gagging. Holding your breath and bearing down (Valsalva manoeuvre). Immersing your face with very cold water while VERY gently pressing on your closed eyes (dive reflex). Steve Mensing developed a variation of this technique which some people report as being very helpful (10).

Coughing, humming and singing can reset things. Chanting 'OM' for example. Possibly these work in a similar way to that of vagal manoeuvres and diaphragmatic breathing as shown in the Roemheld chapter. There have been a few studies on the effects of 'OM' chanting. The idea is that the vibrations through the auricular branch of the vagus nerve, produce limbic deactivation. (Limbic = The limbic system is the part of the brain that has three main functions: emotions, memories and arousal.) For information on 'Om' chanting, visit IJoy Int Journal of Yoga – 2011 (11)

Listening to soothing and relaxing music: "The Potential therapeutic effects of music listening have been largely attributed to its ability to reduce stress and modulate arousal levels. Listening to 'relaxing music' (generally considered to have a slow temp, low pitch and no lyrics) has been shown to reduce stress and anxiety in healthy subjects, patients undergoing medical procedures (e.g., surgery, colonoscopy, dental procedures, paediatric patients undergoing medical procedures and patients with coronary heart disease)." International Journal of Recent Trends in Science and Technology (12)

If you have found other useful tools that we are unaware of, please visit our Facebook group (1) and let us know.

The Vagus Nerve

Dr Rane explained that "The vagus nerve, also referred to as the 10th cranial nerve, is appropriately termed a "mixed" nerve. It provides a sort of two-way communication of nerve impulses back and forth between the brain and the pharynx, larynx, oesophagus, stomach and associated abdominal viscera (basically, your throat, windpipe, your tummy and guts), the heart, lungs and several more complex but irrelevant body organs or functions. The vagus nerve is the longest and most complex of the cranial nerves in the body.

The key point here is to make note that this nerve involves the "heart," the "lungs" and basically the whole digestive system of your tummy and intestines. Now let's pair that with some real specific and limited physiology about the heart and its rhythm. The heart has a natural pacemaker called the sinoatrial node among several less distinct and similar pacers, whose steady rhythmic signals can be affected by which nerve? You guessed it; The VAGUS nerve.

Among its many duties, the vagus nerve helps transfer signals within the parasympathetic nervous system to the brain to regulate the heart in addition to other functions taking place and is doing its job right now in each and every one of us.

Heart Races - Sympathetic Nervous System
Heart Slows Down - Parasympathetic

Think of the nervous system as a two-way street, one being the sympathetic nervous system that sort of represents stepping on the gas pedal, and the parasympathetic nervous system that is analogous to stepping on the brakes so to speak. When your heart races, think sympathetic nervous system and when it slows down, think of the parasympathetic system. " (3)

Reading this helped me to understand that generally, benign palpitations are related to the nervous system and therefore, not directly to the health of the heart. I recognised that I had other symptoms which I had not married up to the palpitations. Once I understood the role of the vagus nerve, a new understanding took hold. Here are a few of my other symptoms:

- Dizzy spells and a spacey feeling, made worse under fluorescent lighting
- Acid Reflux and Oesophageal Spasms
- IBS and nervous stomach
- Inability to take deep breaths (sometimes)
- A sudden dump of adrenaline for no apparent reason causing panic and anxiety attacks
- Heart pounding, missing beats, beating fast and beating slowly

The dizzy spells were and still are intermittent and come on suddenly. I felt worse when in my kitchen which I later realized was initiated by the fluorescent lighting in there.

Fluorescent lighting can trigger nervous system events, such as seizures in those photo sensitives who are susceptible. As most know, this is because of rapid light to dark flickering in fluorescent lighting. Camera flashes and cinema screens can also cause dizziness – anything where light and dark flashes in and out. Bright lights can also trigger spacey feelings for me, as well as palpitations and nervousness.

Dr Rane states: "Remember that we said the vagus nerve is linked to both the tummy, the throat and the heart. Let's assume that we've eaten a meal and it's caused us to experience some gastrointestinal discomfort, or in other words, gas. The irregular presence and activity by your tummy and intestines stimulates, more appropriately irritates, the vagus nerve which sends a rather inappropriate signal back along the pathway to guess where? That's right! The heart...

The vagus nerve stimulates many areas of the body in response to our environment or internal conditions caused by the outside environment, i.e. a meal that produces indigestion. The vagus nerve provides all of us with a stable process called vagal tone. This tone or stability keeps us in a state of physiological preparedness with relation to our environment.

In response to environmental cues or situations, that tone or stability changes to prepare for what may be required. You've probably all seen a guy (or gal) that makes your heart "skip a beat." Ever wonder why that phrase ever came about? Think for a moment. If you've ever been emotionally overcome, your heart races or feels like it pounds in your chest, we begin sweating, our blood pressure rises, we feel nervous and at some point, our face is overcome by a warm flushing sensation that we attribute to nervousness or embarrassment. Well, guess what nerve plays a very big role in that entire process? Right Again!!! The VAGUS nerve. And epinephrine is right there to assist in the process." (3)

Fascinatingly, Vagus Nerve Stimulation Therapy is a new treatment used for some with epilepsy. This involves a small electrical pacemaker like device being implanted under the skin in the chest. The device sends electrical impulses to the brain through the vagus nerve. This can stimulate the vagus nerve to help reduce the number of seizures a person has. Even more fascinating, known side effects include palpitations, difficulty swallowing and stomach discomfort. Also cough, sore throat and shortness of breath. This could mean that something similar is happening to some, if not most of us. It's as though the vagus nerve is being biologically stimulated in a similar way to that of the implanted, pacemaker like device.

The Acid reflux and oesophageal spasms, nervous stomach and IBS, the inability to take deep breaths at times, the panic and anxiety attacks and arrhythmias, all being part of that same process. It is my hope that this idea of the mass of symptoms on top of or as well as palpitations, fuels interest and further research.

Sadly, there are very few research papers that cover the entire list of reported symptoms. Each symptom seems to be isolated as a study on its own, rather than a conglomeration of all symptoms presented. For example, for your heart palpitations, you will be referred to a cardiologist – which is correct. However, once any heart condition is ruled out, any other symptoms are not gathered together to form an idea that might result in a different a condition, perhaps one that has yet to be found.

A specialist in a field relating to one, isolated symptom could read this and make light of it, doing so without thoroughly researching the huge potential for realising an entirely new way of looking at people who present with benign, yet life changing palpitations which are not isolated, but part of a set of symptoms. I am proposing a more holistic approach; one that involves all of the symptoms and one that searches for a common denominator.

I do not want to undermine the role of the cardiologist. A cardiologist should be the first port of call. Cardiologists' are experts on the anatomy of the heart and how it works in conjunction with the rest of the body. A cardiologist can order tests and decipher them to either confirm or rule out heart issues. They are able to refer a person to an electrophysiologist who may perform further tests in relation to the electrical activity of your heart. My message is not ruling out the cardiologist, in fact I feel it is Cardiology, with consultants like Sanjay Gupta (8), who will lead the way forward, along with neurology, endocrinology, gastroenterology and psychology.

I believe inflammation plays a role in all maladies. Currently, inflammation is being attributed to many conditions, from Alzheimer's to aging with newer ideas being talked about and published regularly. There has been some speculation that some forms of depression involve inflammation. (13 and 14)

Inflammation is a response from the body, sending white blood cells to fight and protect us from infection and bacteria and so on. Autoimmune disease is when this response attacks our own, healthy cells. A simple way to explain it is that our immune system becomes confused and turns on us. Could there be any link to inflammation and the symptoms presented?

I am of the mind that although stress may be a precursor to heart palpitations, the opposite can also be said. Palps cause an enormous amount of stress, and stress can cause an inflammatory response. This dampens down the immune system, leaving us vulnerable to infection and other maladies. After four years of constant palps, I developed polymyalgia Rheumatica; an autoimmune disease whereby my immune system attacks my muscle cells.

Science News published an article titled: How stress influences disease: Study reveals inflammation as the culprit - 2012 (15). The paper reviews research undertaken by Carnegie Mellon University's Sheldon Cohen, who found that "chronic psychological stress is associated with the body losing its ability to regulate the inflammatory response."

The article states: "Cohen argued that prolonged stress alters the effectiveness of cortisol to regulate the inflammatory response because it decreases tissue sensitivity to the hormone. Specifically, immune cells become insensitive to cortisol's regulatory effect. In turn, runaway inflammation is thought to promote the development and progression of many diseases.

Cohen, whose ground-breaking early work showed that people suffering from psychological stress are more susceptible to developing common colds, used the common cold as the model for testing his theory. With the common cold, symptoms are not caused by the virus they are instead a "side effect" of the inflammatory response that is triggered as part of the body's effort to fight infection. The greater the body's inflammatory response to the virus, the greater is the likelihood of experiencing the symptoms of a cold."

Although I cannot quite define how this sits with our condition, I have a nagging feeling, as though long before the palps appeared, there was a disposition to them. I arrive at a missing link when I try to dissect the progression from health to palps. On a gut level I am drawn to the idea of stress and inflammation playing a huge role.

In the next chapter I discuss Roemheld Syndrome, which I believe will link to the above symptoms and the idea of irritation and inflammation and its impact on the vagus nerve. For some, Roemheld Syndrome might be the key that unlocks much more research. If research can be taken to higher levels, I feel sure we will gain understanding, cures and/or better management of arrhythmias.

Roemheld Syndrome

Roemheld syndrome first came to my attention when trawling the web for clues to my own palpitations. I had realised that they appeared when I had acid reflux, which at that time was almost all of the time. I came across a podcast of a Radio Programme about RS. Sadly, the podcast was taken off-line a few years later. Luckily, I saved it to 'my box' account (16), which I will gladly share a link to in the reference section at the back of this book. I think it might be helpful to write a little synopsis about what was discussed:

The programme was aired by Superhuman Radio and hosted by Carl Lanore (16).

Carl had invited Dr Mike Smith to talk with him about Roemheld Syndrome. Carl had experienced the syndrome after a course of amoxicillin. He noticed his digestion had stopped functioning efficiently and that he was always bloated and had heart arrhythmia. He found that laying on his left side could also set off the symptoms. He recounted a time when he went to the gym a few hours after eating a particularly large meal. He did some scrunches and when he stood up, his heart went crazy and he was dizzy. He took himself to ER. They gave him a benzo, implying it was anxiety.

Dr Smith said that it is quite common to get this diagnosis because when we present at the doctor's office with heart symptoms, the doctor will do tests for the heart and when they all come back fine, the doctor will assume anxiety. Interestingly, Dr Smith said that he was trained to always think of one organ removed; meaning he thought doctors should think about the organs near to the heart.

Carl mentioned a time when after eating a large breakfast, he stood up and felt dizzy. He began researching and came across information on the vagus nerve and how it regulates the heart rate. More researched helped him learn why, when he was bloated, his stomach pressed against the diaphragm and pinched his vagus nerve.

Dr Smith explained how the parasympathetic nervous system calms us down after stress. When we digest, it is stimulated to slow everything else down. He explained the pressure on the diaphragm, pinches the vagus nerve, which is also, ironically, responsible for digestion. He said it stops the secretion of acid needed for digestion, which creates a vicious circle of bloating, vagus stimulation, poor digestion and more bloating. He, like Carl, mentioned a host of other symptoms which the patient may not link to the heart arrhythmia because the patient is concentrating on the scariest symptom: the heart. He lists a few that may be of interest to you, if you suspect RS: Dizzy spells, bright flashing lights, ringing in the ears, muscle cramps or sharp pain in the lower chest and gastro coronary reflex which he explained is a response from the vagus, trying to slow everything down and the heart, trying to rev everything up.

The whole programme concentrates on Roemheld Syndrome and is compatible with all the other information I have found.

Dr. Smith and Carl offer some alternative things to try as follows:

Digestive enzymes, or eat natural enzymes with foods like pineapple and papaya, after a meal

Burp as much as possible or take something that will help break up the gas and therefore relieve the pressure

Test yourself for food intolerances – remove suspect foods

Refine your diet and try a lower calorie intake (Ludwig Roemheld was studying calorie intake and its effects when he discovered Roemheld Syndrome).

Carl suggested there could be a link to the way we are physically built (something I wonder about – do some of us have less distance between our stomach and our heart?)

Stretching exercises to elevate the diaphragm

Ingest more magnesium either via a supplement or via food.

They did not mention the breathing exercises designed by Bad Wildungen (17) which I will refer to a bit further on.

I would encourage people to listen to the whole programme and decide for themselves if what it has to say, applies to you.

My next step was to search for the term Roemheld Syndrome in the library and on the internet. Much of the information I found had been written in German; some of which I managed to have translated. A kind German author sent me a PDF of his book "Roemheld Syndrome" to enable me to translate it into English using google translate.

Roemheld Syndrome was first described by Ludwig von Roemheld (1871 – 1938). It was first named Roemheld-Techlenburg-Ceconi-Syndrome, or Roemheld Gastric Cardiac syndrome. It has since been shortened and often referred to simply as: RS. If searching for information on the internet, also type in the words gastro-cardia and gastric-cardia.

Roemheld Syndrome links a number of conditions in the gastrointestinal tract to the following symptoms:

- Angina pectoris
- Anxiety
- Vertigo or dizziness
- Cramp
- Difficulty inhaling
- Fatigue
- Hot flashes
- Left ventricular discomfort
- Palpitations / Ectopic beats
- Poor perfusion
- Sinus bradycardia
- Uncomfortable breathing
- Sleep apnoea or sleep disturbances

You can see these are very similar to my own symptoms mentioned earlier.

The causes could be any of the following:

- Gall bladder issues
- Acute pancreatic necrosis
- The inability to belch
- Cardiac bridge (Coronary occluding reflexes triggered by coronary reflexes)
- Food poisoning
- Excessive gas in the transverse colon caused by:
- Gall stones
- Gastroesophageal reflux disease
- Hiatal hernia
- Lactose intolerance
- Sphincter dysfunction
- Silent Reflux
- Air swallowing

In 1984, Bad Wildungen gave a lecture at workshops for the Task force of Clinical Psychologists in Heath Resorts, Section Clinical Psychology BDP (German Association of Psychologists), and The Psychologist Task Force Autogenic Training and Progressive Relaxation. The talk was on "Breathing Exercises for Roemheld Syndrome". The lecture was documented and is available in PDF form. I will leave a link to this paper (17) because it proposes a cure and if not cure, then management of the syndrome.

Roemheld Syndrome or RS for short, appears to be more popular in the medical community in Germany. Here in the UK, and I believe the US, it less thought about. Many of us find that some of our doctors pay little attention to the idea, nor do they tend to ask about any associated stomach issues or the possibility or tests/scans to look at heart displacement or elevation of the diaphragm.

Wildungen quotes the Psychyremble Clinical dictionary which "defines it briefly" as follows:

"Displacement of the heart toward the upper right side as a consequence of an elevated diaphragm (mostly commonly on the left side) due to bloating of stomach and/or intestines"

He goes on to describe symptoms as: "Cardiac problems, extra systoles, stomach pains, nausea and even stenocardiac attacks." (stenocardia attacks are a sudden shortage of oxygen in the heart due to narrowing – this would be picked up during an echo and/or stress test I believe)

It is interesting that Bad Wildungen was a psychologist. He tells us that many of his patients came because of gastrointestinal problems, and that 90% of those patients also had cardiac problems which they did not mention, having previously not been taken seriously. This leads me to assume that patients were referred to him because there was a suspicion that the gastro and cardiac problems were psychosomatic in nature. Perhaps, and I am guessing, with a diagnosis of anxiety.

He states:

"Many of these patients did not come to me because of cardiac problems, but because of gastrointestinal problems. Many of them had not even listed their cardiac problems because they had learned they would not be taken seriously. In discussions with colleagues and physicians at the University Clinic of Bonn, who are members of the procedural task force, which I am also part of, I came away with the impression that of the patients at the hospital who have functional cardiac problems, at least 50%, if not considerably more have RS."

This left Wildungen convinced that RS is much more common than previously assumed. From this he developed breathing exercises which he proposed would lessen or even cure Roemheld Syndrome. I will go into this in more detail later, however, I do recommend you download and read the paper so that you may try the breathing exercises for yourself. They take only 25 minutes of your day, in 5, 5-minute bursts. At the point of writing, I am about to give them a whirl myself.

In 2014, the WJG (World Journal of Gastroenterology) published a study titled: Atrial fibrillation in patients with gastroesophageal reflux disease: A comprehensive review. (18)

The aim of the study was to analyse the potential relationship of GERD and the development of AF. Their method was to screen relevant publications on GERD and AF in adults between Jan 1972 and Dec 2013. While this paper looks mainly at AF, it can be translated using the same mechanism for people who suffer from palps. It is unfortunate that "Studies written in languages other than English and French," were not included in the review. This will mean that many papers on Roemheld Syndrome will not have been studied because most of them are written in German. However, much of the material mentioned seems to have overtones of the same nature as RS.

Their results were as follows:

"Two thousand one hundred and sixty-one titles were found of which 8 articles met the inclusion criteria. The presence of AF in patients with GERD was reported to be between 0.62% - 14% higher compared to those without GERD. Epidemiology data provided by the observational studies showed that patients with GERD, especially those with more severe GERD related symptoms, had an increased risk of developing AF, compared with those without GERD, but a causal relationship between GERD and AF could not be established based on these studies. The mechanisms of AF as a consequence of GERD remain largely unknown, with inflammation and vagal stimulation playing a possible role in the development of these disorders. Treatment with proton pump inhibitors may improve symptoms related to AF and facilitate conversion to sinus rhythm."

This paper, and indeed many others, recognise that GERD alone can make life very difficult, let alone arrhythmia relating to the GERD. There is no denial that GERD can cause palpitations, AF, SVT and so on. I am in GERD groups on Facebook and many people report missed and skipped beats when suffering from reflux. The reviewed articles all agree that GERD is often the culprit and PPI's if tolerable can ease the problem, if not fix it. However, once again we see them documented as two separate problems, with one issue causing another.

In my opinion, the relationship between acid, inflammation and/or irritation of the vagus nerve in many cases, is part of a wider problem. The difficulty might be that a symptom is often taken at face value; a cough is the respiratory system; the stomach is the gastro system and so on. As an example, I have an acquaintance who had a constant tickly cough. Her doctor was baffled, having quite rightly ordered an X-ray which showed no sign of anything that might cause the cough. Eventually the cough went away when she saw a new doctor who suggested she may have silent reflux and who prescribed a PPI. Her previous doctor referred her to a pulmonary specialist. The referral was right and proper; however, I am trying to highlight that there can be many roads to diagnosis with some leading to dead ends. Just because the symptom does not have an obvious cause, does not mean there is no cause.

Another interesting paper I came across was one published in 2005 by The Texas Heart Institute Journal) titled: Delugation-Induced Atrial Fibrillation (19). It is an extraordinary, yet short paper of a case report involving "a 38-year-old woman who presented at outpatient clinic with 4 days of intermittent palpitations up to 30 times a day, each episode lasting for a few seconds…Each of these episodes was associated with eating. She denied any symptoms of heartburn, dysphagia (difficulty swallowing), or odynophagia (pain on swallowing)."

The patient was treated with medications which she was subsequently weaned from and continued to be free from symptoms for the 5 years between her treatment and the writing of the paper. In the "Discussion" section of the paper, the authors state that "Swallowing induced dysrhythmias are divided into essentially two categories – bradyrhythmias and tachyrhythmias, the former being the more common than the latter. Most cases of swallowing induced bradyrhythmias are a variety of antrioventricular block and are associated with either an oesophageal abnormality or coronary artery disease. Tachyrhythmias induced by swallowing are infrequent, are commonly described as atrial tachycardia rather than as true atrial fibrillation and are generally not associated with oesophageal disease."

There is a brief discussion on a theory that "hypothesises mechanical stimulation of the left atrium by the distended oesophagus." Some negating arguments to this hypothesis are considered, although the writers show that "The most striking feature was the significant difference in amplitude in the distal oesophagus between wet swallows (all of which were associated with atrial fibrillation) and dry swallows (half of which were not associated with atrial fibrillation) (70 vs 26mmHG). Although no meaningful pressure tracing could be recorded with dry swallows that caused atrial fibrillation, one can infer from the above findings that intraoesophageal pressure that exceeds a certain threshold can trigger atrial fibrillation." They go on to say: "The mechanism for initiating of tachycardia, as proved by our case, is vasovagal reflex. The afferent and efferent branches of the vagus nerve are activated during a rise in the intraoesopageally pressure. Preferential vagal discharge to the atrial myocardium, rather than to the sinus node, could result in atrial ectopic activity…"

The authors have been quite thorough in their observations and present an interesting case which I believe has room for more investigation. They admit that "an explanation of the phenomenon remains unclear."

In trying to compare my own symptoms to that of the 38-year-old patient above, I recognise the lady in question reported no heartburn or difficulty swallowing, whereas I have severe heartburn which often leads me to have difficulty swallowing. Could this mean that gas or air pressure was the cause of her AF? Could she have had an elevated diaphragm which created pressure when she swallowed?

This brings me back to my idea of GERD being but one malady and that all symptoms may be gathered together as indicators of a cause; that of Roemheld Syndrome. Even more than this, I want to understand what actually causes RS. Wildungen (17) puts forward that "the model has three distinct features:

1: an overfilled/bloated stomach
2: an elevated diaphragm
3: pressure on and/or displacement of the heart"

He proposes that; "A functional analysis of these three distinct features raises at least the following questions:

1: What is overfill of the stomach?
2: How can the diaphragm which is a muscle, become permanently elevated? What went wrong here?"

Feature 3 is simply the result of feature 1 and 2: If pressure is exerted on the heart, no matter how, or from which direction, it will react in some way: with pain, stabbing or other, extrasystoles, tachycardia, bradycardia, a feeling of tightness or other."

He goes on to explain that the stomach can become overfilled with food, but also with air that is swallowed when eating. He thinks this has to do with "breathing without sufficiently involving the diaphragm." He proposes that people with RS tend to use auxiliary muscles when breathing rather than diaphragmatic breathing and describes it as an untrained, elevated diaphragm which gets pushed upward toward the heart. He suggests that it is quite common for people with RS to have digestive issues. His paper includes diagrams and extensive explanations, as mentioned previously, for better breathing. He proposes that the reintroduction of diaphragmatic breathing suppresses all Roemheld Syndrome symptoms.

Since Wildungen's lecture, there has been a steady growth of ideas about breathing and wrong or shallow breathing. Yoga U published a wonderful paper titled: Tapping into the Power of the Vagus Nerve – How Your Breath Can Change Your Relationships, written by B Grace Bullock PHD who proposes that "You can change your experience by changing your breath." This is an extraordinary piece of writing and I recommend everyone read it if they want to understand more about the relationship between psychology, breathing and vagal tone. (20)

You may have heard of 2 to 1 breathing. As it is free to try, perhaps check out the following article on Yoga International's website - Soothe Your Nervous System with 2-to-1 Breathing by John Clarke, MD (21)

There are a huge number of articles, papers and you tube videos on correct and healing breathing. One other I would like to mention, which may appeal to TED Talk listeners, is a YouTube Video called "Breath to Heal" by Max Strom. Max talks briefly about hidden mental anguish which he says converts to physical symptoms, in particular the anguish of grief. He also demonstrates the 4-7-8 breath technique which can help with stress and anxiety. This really does help to calm everything down and rebalance. (22)

Wildungen's (17) ideas on an "overfilled/bloated stomach, an elevated diaphragm and pressure on and/or displacement of the heart" might explain the regular reports within our Facebook group that palps can be set off by posture alone: bending forward, laying or leaning on the left side, lifting arms, especially the left arm and being bent over the computer. On very sensitive days people say that even talking can cause palps. It also goes along with the regular feedback that belching can often relieve palps and SVT. I personally can recognise the buildup of air in my oesophagus. I find walking tends to relieve this, especially walking after a meal. I wonder if by doing this, I am allowing a distance between the stomach and the heart while digesting? More intense studies might generate the answer.

I want to mention something I have noticed when I am stressed. I suffer from involuntary swallowing. It is a little like the exaggerated gulp we see when people are nervous. If I have a very stressful day I tend to gulp air. In the early days I knew if I had a stressful day, I would surly have palps for the following three days. It was not until I came across Wildungen's paper that I linked the air gulping to the palps.

The European Society of Cardiology published a paper titled: Atrial fibrillation and gastroesophageal reflux disease: the cardiogastric integration 2017 (23), in which they state:

"Interestingly, in patients with GERD, episodes of GERD, triggered by defaecation, abdominal bloating (as with RS), cold water, fatty food consumption (so called prandial or triggered AF) were reported."

It is my belief that although this paper looks at the relationship of stomach and AF, the same mechanisms apply with palpitations. The authors make reference to Ludwig Roemheld, acknowledging him to be the first to describe the relationship between gastrointestinal symptoms and arrhythmias. They describe the anatomical atrial – oesophageal relationship:

"The posterior wall of the left atrium and the oesophagus are separated by a tissue layer of only ~5 mm. The exact anatomical relationship between oesophagus and Atrium is not fixed. It has been reported that oesophagus location is different in computer tomography scans before procedure and during contrast oesophagogram during procedure. In some patients, oesophagus is close to left pulmonary vein, while others are close to right pulmonary vein. Oesophageal vessels and lymph nodes as well as paraesophageal nerve plexus are located within the tissue layer. The paraesophageal nerve plexus regulates the motility of the stomach and can branch above or below the level of the left atrium."

This might explain why DGL and Aloe Vera used by GERD sufferers can often calm palps if they are induced by oesophageal spasms because they act as natural anti-inflammatories. DGL can protect the oesophagus and gut and perhaps stop the 5mm tissue layer from being saturated with stomach acid. It would make sense therefore, to research supplements or medicines that might protect and/or strengthen gastric mucosa, which is approximately 1mm thick. Gastric mucosa's purpose is to lubricate, ensuring the smooth movement of food, and to protect and act as a barrier.

The paper includes MRI images showing the relationship between the oesophagus and the posterior wall of the left atrium. I think this article, along with other papers published, generally in Europe and specifically Germany, present a more up to date version of RS. While the paper being discussed mentions cardiac perfusion, hiatus hernia, inflammatory bowel disease and coeliac disease – for the purpose of this book, I am drawn to the mechanisms and relationship between stomach and palpitations, AF and GERD.

The paper goes explains Autonomic activation:

"Neural reflex arcs from the oesophagus and the heart have been shown in both animals and humans. In humans, chemical, electrical and mechanical stimulation of the Oesophagus modifies the sympathovagal balance. Oesophageal stimulation amplifies respiratory-driven cardiac vagoafferent modulation. Oesophageal acid stimulation is further associated with an increase in vagal activity. Acid refluxes cause a local inflammatory process that may directly alter the autonomic innervations of the oesophageal mucosa and may penetrate the oesophageal wall and stimulate the adjacent vagal nerves. Injury to the distal oesophagus can further impair vagal nerve responses, particularly nerve sensitisation of the afferent pathways. These and other considerations suggest the involvement of the cardio-oesophagael reflex in case of GERD associated AF."

As previously mentioned; inflammation seems currently quite buzzy in terms of its relationship to a variety of maladies, with more information about it popping up on a regular basis. The following excerpt from the paper seems to compound that idea:

"Propagation of the local inflammatory process through the oesophageal wall may also cause local pericarditis or atrial myocarditis due to the proximity of the oesophagus to the left atrium...circulating inflammatory cytokines have been shown to play a role in the pathophysiology of AF. Inflammation of the oesophageal mucosa affects local receptors that may induce afferent – efferent reflex mechanisms."

The paper concludes that: "clinicians should be aware of the possible cardiogastric interaction with GERD being associated with AF. Identification and appropriate treatment of GERD, especially oesophagitis, may help to reduce AF onset and symptoms and can facilitate conversion from AF to sinus rhythm in subsets of patients. Further prospective and well-designed studies are needed."

It is my personal experience with medical professionals here in the UK, and with feedback from many of the Facebook group members from all over the world, who recount their interactions with their doctors, with the exception of a few, like Sanjay Gupta, there seems little recognition of the gastrocardiac connection. Approximately 80% of people who visit the FB group report palps with associated GERD. Remembering our lesson from Dr Rane, that "the vagus nerve helps transfer signals within the parasympathetic nervous system to the brain to regulate the heart in addition to other functions," it makes sense that we suffer not only palpitations, but a host of other symptoms.

In this sense, more recognition of the distress caused by heart irregularities and accompanying symptoms is needed, as well as more investigative research into solutions. While PPI's have been shown to reduce and even stop symptoms – they are not a long-term solution. PPI's are not always well tolerated and I have personal experience of this. Even when they are, they come with their own long-term risks.

I have seen no mention in any of the papers relating to the gastro – cardiac connection, of the operation mentioned earlier; Nissen Fundoplication, which tightens the lower oesophageal sphincter by wrapping the upper part of the stomach, around the lower end of the oesophagus. Perhaps this could be more successful in the long term, however I wonder if it also has the potential to worsen things. Without appropriate research we are unable to take a guess.

There are newer approaches and treatments for the problem: discussed in a paper by Robert A Ganz MD: A Review of New Surgical and Endoscopic Therapies for Gastroesophageal Reflux Disease: He tells us about "New surgical techniques include sphincter augmentation of the LES using a magnetic implant that encircles the native LES (LINX, Torax Medical), which is available in the United States and Europe, and a surgically implanted LES pacemaker (EndoStim, EndoStim BV) that is currently available only in Europe." (24)

Disappointingly, newer techniques are not yet widely available. Largely due to lack of study and training. An abstract from the paper states:

"Treatment of gastroesophageal reflux disease in the United States today is binary, with the majority of patients with gastroesophageal reflux disease being treated with antisecretory medications and a minority of patients, typically those with volume regurgitation, undergoing Nissen fundoplication. However, there has been increasing dissatisfaction with proton pump inhibitor therapy among a significant number of patients with gastroesophageal reflux disease owing to cost, side effects, and refractory symptoms, and there has been a general reluctance to undergo surgical fundoplication due to its attendant side-effect profile. As a result, a therapy gap exists for many patients with gastroesophageal reflux disease. Alternative techniques are available for these gap patients, including 2 endoscopic fundoplication techniques, an endoscopic radiofrequency energy delivery technique, and 2 minimally invasive surgical procedures. These alternative techniques have been extensively evaluated; however, there are limitations to published studies, including arbitrary definitions of success, variable efficacy measurements, deficient reporting tools, inconsistent study designs, inconsistent lengths of follow-up postintervention, and lack of comparison data across techniques. Although all of the techniques appear to be safe, the endoscopic techniques lack demonstrable reflux control and show variable symptom improvement and variable decreases in proton pump inhibitor use. The surgical techniques are more robust, with evidence for adequate reflux control, symptom improvement, and decreased proton pump inhibitor use; however, these techniques are more difficult to perform and are more intrusive. Additionally, these alternative techniques have only been studied in patients with relatively normal anatomy. The field of gastroesophageal reflux disease treatment is in need of consistent definitions of efficacy, standardized study design and outcome measurements, and improved reporting tools before the role of these techniques can be fully ascertained."

I am aware that a lot of my discussion has centred around Gastro-cardiac ideas and RS. I think this is because I have become increasingly aware of how many members using our Facebook group mention stomach issues of one kind or another. For those who cannot relate to gastro issues, you might still be interested in the concept that inflammation and irritation of the vagus nerve have the potential to be possible culprits of your palps and that a form of RS could still be possible. Whether Palps are born from medication, autoimmune disease, pregnancy, and all the other things mention in the 'Why Palps – Why me?" chapter, autonomic messaging appears to be confused.

I am not discounting electrophysiology and its study of the electrical activity in the heart and of procedures such as ablation. What I write is not to dispute these studies and procedures, or to imply there is no need for them. What I am suggesting is that a full study of any malady, should, I believe, include a study of the whole person and his/her range of physical symptoms.

While in hospital as an inpatient, it was suggested to me that I have an ablation, which for me with a particular blood condition could be risky. It was also suggested that I go on blood thinners. I have a familial, severe blood platelet condition and the type of blood thinner I was offered has irreversible side effects, therefore, if I were to haemorrhage, it could have dire consequences for me. Luckily, I had prior knowledge about this drug in relation to my blood/bone marrow condition, which was later reiterated by my haematologist who was quite clear that I am not to be prescribed blood thinners. I mention this because I believe we are all different and unique. We are not a symptom, or a set of symptoms – we are people, often in distress and in need of the type of medical attention that looks at the whole person; as a new puzzle, not a general one which when completed reveals the same picture.

Update: It has come to my attention that there is now an antidote for the newer blood thinners. However, for me, blood thinner is still not viable due to my malfunctioning and low numbers of blood platelets. The criteria presented to me which was used to evaluate my need for a blood thinner, I believe was and is flawed in that it does not take into consideration low platelet counts and other bleeding conditions. However, in my case, once the doctor concerned was presented with the facts of my condition, it was agreed not to prescribe a blood thinner.

The Loss of Self

"Death is not the greatest loss in life.
The greatest loss is what dies inside
us while we live."

Norman Cousins

The idea of loss may not apply to all. I have seen many people report that they manage quite well and have learned to ignore their palps much of the time. When I read this, it pleases me. But, I am often left wondering several things: Do they have them as severely as some of us? Do they become dizzy like many of us do? Do they have lots of support? And so on. I then review myself thinking perhaps I am a failure or should be stronger. Finally, I conclude that whatever the reason, I can only be with how I am, and that means not beating myself up when I am frightened. I accept that feeling frightened is how it is for me. It may be this is how it is for you. If it is, I want you to know that you are not alone; there are thousands of us, possibly millions. Fear, in my estimation arrives without thought in the first instance. It is as though the body reacts to a threat automatically; a primal reflex perhaps.

For people with young children, it is not uncommon for them to report that they feel bereft at the loss of enjoying their child or children as they would want to. Perhaps feeling their mind is only half involved because they are using the other half of their energy to control the fear and anxiety the palps are creating, ironically, so they can care for their children.

Here is a list of reported losses:

- Driving
- Socialising
- Enjoying children
- Holidays and Trips
- Exercise
- Friends (lost or changed)
- Relationships (lost or changed)
- Inviting guests to your home
- Being a guest
- Job
- Self esteem
- Joy
- Trust in the process of life
- Finances

Perhaps the list seems simple at a glance. But each loss will have a huge story in front of and behind it, and therefore, its meaning is far from simple because one loss leads to so many. For example: If you can no longer drive because your particular palps cause light headedness or dizziness, it could mean that you are unable to get to your place of work, which might lead to you losing or leaving your job. This in turn could cause financial problems and even relationship difficulties and so on.

For many of us, experiencing the skips and jumps, thuds, pauses, flutters and more, can be truly traumatic. To be in a state of fight or flight for hours, even days on end is unnerving, disrupting and upsetting. Crying, getting angry, feeling worn out, nervous, fearful for minutes, hours, days and even months describes many of our lives.

Not always but often, people report exasperation from partners, friends and family. "you have been told they are harmless," they may say. Others may say nothing but there is sometimes a sense of criticism in their silence. As with all invisible illness, some people can think you are being dramatic or hypochondriacal, or even that you may be putting it on. You might feel like a burden or lesser person. Maybe you see less and less of friends because such a big part of you is unavailable. You are a victim of these awful, whacky beats and you can feel trapped in your body and let down by it. Continued palps can wipe out your confidence. Some of you are more able to stand up and be counted, however in general, these things weaken your sense of self. You might experience envy toward those who go about their life without experiencing what we palpers experience. Seeing people travelling, flying, laughing, socialising and living life to the full when you are living in fear can be painful. Even if you have good days, it can be terrifying to plan a social outing because most of us come to learn that palps can strike at any time. This form or agoraphobia is most distressing.

There are degrees of agoraphobia. Some people cannot leave the safety of their home. Others can manage to move about in their safe zones, or comfort zones. This means they may manage the anxiety enough to venture out to the local shop, or to post a letter or someplace nearby and well known. There will be internal rehearsals on how they might deal with palps and panic if they happen while they are out. Oftentimes, the agoraphobia begins with one incident; an incident which the mind has not processed and we might refer to this as post-traumatic stress. There are therapies that can help enormously with this type of agoraphobia. I knew of someone who had been outside in the street when she had a miscarriage. It involved lots of blood, collapse and an ambulance. I guess you can work out why she developed agoraphobia. With therapy, she did recover and was once again able to go out. However, the type of agoraphobia we palpers develop is continual. It does not stem from a past experience; it is very current and ongoing. To put it succinctly: I do not fear outside of me – I fear inside of me.

Another aspect of this type of agoraphobia is the dread of embarrassment. I personally have felt embarrassed on a few occasions when I have felt faint or dizzy while walking along and have had to hang on to a wall. One time in a supermarket, I pulled down a display of breakfast cereal when I felt faint and instinctively reached out for the nearest support. People stared, and I felt self-conscious and alone. We can argue or discuss society and that perhaps the fault lays there. But, it is what it is and even if we are victims of a harsh society, knowing that does not help and sometimes when leaving the home to be outside, in that society, we fear the feeling of shame.

The kind of fear and loss many of us suffer is heartbreaking, and so little acknowledged by the medical profession and researchers. The support we need is not available and all we have is each other. We feel as though we have two options: continue to research ourselves and our condition and do the best we can to find things to manage our symptoms, or come to terms with our changed, restricted and shallow lives.

My heart breaks every time I read of someone's distress. It breaks for them and it breaks for me. I feel good when I read that people have found solutions and am full of praise for those who continue to support others. Mostly, when people do heal, we no longer see them visiting the Facebook group and that is okay; they have been lost and then found. For those of us who have been dealing with long term palps, SVT and AF, there is a sense of weariness. It is as though we cannot find the self we were because we become lost under the debris of a life we once had.

Loss of Trust in the Process of life

We all understand that everything comes to an end, including us. We know we are going to cease living one day – but we humans have a great gift – that of denial. Although I term it a gift, there are times where denial works against us. At some point when we learn about death and dying, in order to survive the anxiety, we tuck thoughts of it away; they are safely hiding in the unconscious where they can do no harm. We live with the idea that death is what happens to other people. Sometimes, life circumstances cause death anxiety to break through those defences, mostly though, we can push them back down again fairly quickly. There are those however, who suffer all the time from this anxiety and these people are unable to keep those thoughts down under. As much as they try, the thoughts keep resurfacing. I think perhaps because denial takes a lot of psychic energy to maintain. People who suffer trauma, especially associated with death, can feel less able to maintain that energy. Sometimes there are things going on in life that are so difficult to deal with, all defence energy is allocated to the management of them. This is like removing the bricks from one wall to build another. Previously hidden thoughts can break through the weakened barrier. If we are using most of our bricks to manage the palps and their impact on us, it makes sense that we begin to experience panic and anxiety not only about death, but about trying to live a normal life too.

Existentially, death, illness and accidents are givens – they happen, and our hearts misbehaving remind us of this on a regular basis. This can wear down and break through our defence mechanisms, sometimes on an hour by hour, or even minute by minute basis. This is similar, I believe, to Post Traumatic Stress, particularly I think for some of us who suffer badly, and/or those of us who also get SVT (Super Ventricular Tachycardia), AFib (Atrial Fibrillation), though not excluding really troublesome Palps alone. Let me explain further:

When people have been in a life-threatening accident, perhaps being badly injured – some tend to recall the scene as a slowing down of time, and many say they thought it was the end for them. In those moments, any denial of death is obliterated as the possibility becomes real. In time and with help, people often recover from that kind of trauma and they either come to terms with it; feeling at peace with the idea of dying, or they may go back into denial. What would happen though, if they were regularly in serious road accidents? This may seem an extreme comparison because we have been told our condition is benign. But does our unconscious fight or flight response understand and call upon that information during the episodes where our hearts are out of rhythm, along with other possible disturbing symptoms, like dizziness or fainting? And, over time, does the whole of our nervous system become so overworked and traumatised that it is acting as it might with PTSD.

Fight or flight as most of us know is the body's response to threat and danger. It is a reaction where hormones like cortisol and adrenaline are released into the blood. Heart rate will increase, you may sweat, your vision narrows and hearing becomes super sensitive. This is not a thought-out process, it is more of a reflex. The sympathetic nervous system alerts the adrenal glands which then release catecholamines - epinephrine (adrenaline), norepinephrine, and dopamine. Catecholamines work as neurotransmitters, sending signals from neuron to neuron, as well as hormones. These regulate your heartbeat and breathing rate, blood pressure and glucose levels. They are signalling the body to get ready for flight or fight. Hence, our already badly-behaved hearts are being stimulated to misbehave even more because ironically, it is an attempting to survive. We can become caught in a cycle of palps – fear – more palps – more fear and so on. There are a few things that may help with this cycle. I find EFT (Emotional Freedom Tapping) great at helping the anxiety wind down. Prana breathing and meditation are very useful. For those like myself who experience a sudden release of adrenaline into the system, which I can verify feels very scary, try actually running on the spot if you are able. This surge is acting as though you are preparing to run, it is giving you the energy, preparing you to survive; so, if able enough, run, even if it is on the spot in your home, and it will disperse.

It is my belief that those of us who experience many palps every day are living in a constant state of stress; we are on the edge waiting to fall. For some, even sleep does not bring peace as many of us are woken by racing or skipping hearts. It can feel as though we want to escape our own bodies. We feel we have lost control over ourselves. Most of all, we no longer relax into life. Our defences are overworked and therefore dysfunctional. If we previously jollied along, trusting in the process and feeling safe in the world, suddenly we come know that anything can interrupt that process and for many, this will mean being in touch with the idea of death, loss of health and fear of illness. Many people report developing heart anxiety and overall health anxiety, fear of taking medications, agoraphobia, claustrophobia (especially in cinemas, theatres, buses, trains and standing in line at checkouts in shops), fear of travel and socialising. The list is huge and pages long. I feel many readers could add a host of other phobias and anxieties.

I have this notion that unless our hearts are sick, perhaps with heart disease or extra electrical pathways etc, medicine needs to take a total view of what is happening to us. For example, to note and marry up other symptoms: are they gastro related, or neurological – are we looking at hormones, stomach, heart, nervous system or all of these? Would this involve a variety of medical professionals making an effort to understand together, rather than us being referred to cardiology alone?

When I mentioned loss in the Facebook group, many members replied and have given me permission to publish some of their comments. I have tried not to edit them too much because I do not wish to change anything, anyone has said. However, my system has changed a few things during spell and grammar checks, as well as changes when uploading to kindle. I have used initials only, for the sake of people's privacy. I want to add my heartfelt thanks for their openness and honesty. The feedback shows in some instances that people have contemplated taking their own lives. If nothing else, I hope this knowledge does encourage professionals, families, friends and associates to understand the seriousness of this condition and I want to further encourage it to be thought of, in some cases, as a disability.

Facebook Group Feedback

SG: TLDR: I'm fine! I just want to share my story. About 10 years ago, while trying to juggle an 18-credit semester and 25-hour part time job, I began to experience heart palpitations. This started a long road of testing, including tilt table tests (where the goal is to get you to faint), 24-hour Holter monitors (basically an EKG that you carry with you all day), echocardiograms, exercise stress tests, etc. Most cardiologists look at a slim 20-something year old and immediately say, "it's anxiety, it's all in your head". I grappled with this idea of being crazy, of having physical symptoms as a product of my own imagination, while trying medicines such as Paxil for panic disorder, Xanax for panic attacks, even Zoloft for a time (an SSRI). Thanks to good insurance, I eventually had enough scary episodes (and enough of feeling crazy) to seek out a specialist in arrhythmia, an electrophysiologist (EP). He caught PVCs (premature ventricular contractions) on a Holter monitor, which are very common and mostly benign for those who have structurally normal hearts (I do). I gave beta blockers a college try, but due to my naturally low blood pressure, they were not a good fit and didn't seem to alleviate my symptoms. Finally, in Sep 2016 I had an EP study, where a catheter is inserted through your groin up to your heart, and a drug is used to stimulate your heart's electrical impulses, with the goal of using ablation to "kill" any spots on the heart where the abnormal rhythms originate. The study unfortunately did not produce enough arrhythmia for me to have an ablation, so afterward I received an implanted cardiac device, a loop monitor, with a battery life of 3 years. Now I can record episodes any time I have them. And I no longer feel crazy! Not only have I recorded PVCs, but I've also recorded PACs, NSVT, SVT, and wide complex tachycardia (hey Dr. Google!). My symptom-producing episodes typically result in panic attacks. Panic disorder (with agoraphobia) makes you avoid situations in which you've had panic attacks before for fear of having them again. There were times I could not drive myself to work. I felt so weak and so embarrassed. I am in a better place now, but I still work at it every day. I just wanted to put this out there because I'm tired of trying to hide it or pretend it doesn't exist, and to say I have such respect for anyone who lives with a chronic condition.

SP: I have been dealing with the dreaded palps/skips/flutters/runs etc... for 1/2 my life. They started at the age of 18 and I was quickly diagnosed with MVP (turns out I don't have it and there is a question if I ever did...back then (1980's) it was a blanket diagnosis for a lot of unexplained cardiac issues). Through my 20s they came and went without many incidents. I did pass out a few times and had many tests done but I was told I was fine. And it wasn't until two years ago when I went through the trauma of losing my father when they reared their ugly head and became pretty much a mainstay of my life.

My losses are huge. Not only did I lose my father I feel as if I lost myself. I have lost friends, isolating myself because I felt safer in my bed than I did in public. I have lost valuable time with my husband, even though he tries to understand these things just have a way of just ruining everything.

I have been through therapy, tests (EVERY test in the book times 2!) I am on my 3rd cardiologist and 2nd soon to be 3rd EP. I know there has to be an answer out there somewhere that is NOT "benign PVCs ...just deal with them..." I want to know the WHY....there HAS to be better treatment. I am SO thankful for this group and the great friends I have made

My hope is we ALL get better management and that the science behind this makes great gains so that the many who suffer, often in silence, isolation, depression, anxiousness and frustration will be recognized for the STRONG people we are.

CDS: I too like SP have dealt with these over half my life 20 years.....all of it...PVC, PAC, bigeminy, couplets, and SVT. You name it. Every other beat literally 2 years straight. Worse now than ever before. Started when I was 20 as well. I have been put on paxil, Lexapro, effexor none of which worked. Zero....I just deal with anxiety and very bad. But I still swear that these things cause my anxiety.

I have been through many jobs trying to find the right one that will "work" with these things...it's horrible. I'm scared to be in a relationship... because they won't understand why I "need a minute" when I'm walking somewhere or why I say "give me a sec" or why I toss and turn before sleep. My kids know when a bad episode kicks in, I can't give them my attention and not paying a word to what they say because I'm worried I'm going to fall over and die at that moment. It's horrible just horrible.

Lastly, hate to bring this up. But I too have had suicide thoughts because this can be just so unbearable to live with...I joke with family who knows about it that if I'm not here I took matters into my own hands. It's truly crippling.

Hate is a strong word but I truly hate these things. I have been in and out the ER many times. Yes, they clearly see them and all they do is up my atenolol.

Truly grateful for this site. I truly believe it has saved me also when it's to the breaking point for me.

AF: These things have taken my life from me. I used to go places. Now I work and come home that's it. Sometimes my husband has to babysit me because the fear is too much. My kids are older now but they've lost the mother that could do things. I have anxiety that I believe I acquired from these things and I take meds but I don't have any freedom. I feel so weighed down and alone. No one understands the crippling fear. I've had these things for the better part of 25 years. Even now I'm laying here afraid to fall asleep. It really sucks.

JL: I've suffered with pvc's, pac's, afib, vt, svt and avnrt for 20 years now. I've had four ablations and they always seem to grow back. It has taken over my life. All the things I did before I was 18 is long gone and I'll never be that person again after suffering from this. For a few years I was a complete agoraphobic. Wouldn't leave my house for anything! I've since got a little better with it and on my good days try to do things because I know my bad days are way more often. I can't be alone because of the overwhelming fear from how this makes me feel and I hate being around crowds, in cars, in big buildings, traffic, so many things I would have never took any notice to before all this started. I feel like I've missed out on so much. It's very depressing. The anxiety alone from these is so debilitating. It's a little more comforting to know there are others out there that feel what I go thru on a daily basis. I'm not the only one

EA: Hi everyone! I'm a bit late to the party but in honor of the seven-year anniversary, I just wanted to say that this group has truly saved my life. I've had PVCs since I was 13, but they were few and far between. When I was 17 they suddenly got much worse and I was taken to the ER, but as I'm sure many of you have experienced, the doctors told me I was fine and made it seem like it was all in my head. I'm 20 now and the last three years have been filled with EKGs, MRIs, ultrasounds, stress tests, and visits to every cardiologist in my area. Eventually I stopped going because I was wasting what little money I had; it was clear no one was ever going to help me. I've tried everything under the sun, biofeedback, vitamins, supplements, atenolol, going to the chiropractor, the list goes on. I've had to quit two jobs. Made one suicide attempt. Lost what I imagine would add up to six months of my life lying in bed and crying with so much rage, hopelessness, loneliness, and anguish. My PCVs are horrible and unrelenting, and there's nothing I can do about them. I'm not as strong as some of you, I can't just ignore them, they completely control every aspect of my life. I go to work and college from home now and I've had to give up so many important things in my life. Thanks to my

PVCs I now have depression and anxiety. I'd give anything in this world to be a normal 20-year-old. My mom found this group for me after my suicide attempt, and it has done wonders. I couldn't believe how many of you had stories identical to mine, and the feeling of not being alone in this hell was indescribable. You guys are some of the kindest, most resilient people I've ever seen, and we are the last people on Earth who deserve to live this way. I'll never be able to live a full life with my PVCs, but they get easier to manage every day, and I owe a lot of it to this group. You guys have all given me a reason to carry on each day with my head held high. Now that I want to stay alive, I'm going to devote it to finding a cure for these horrendous things.

EA: Thank you so much Jen! I don't know what to say! We do all need a voice, we need the world to see us and hear us because what we suffer through each day is invisible to everyone else. We smile and put on a brace face when inside we are trapped in our own personal hell with no way out, and the only people who can help us treat our heart conditions like they're more mental than physical. Just because they won't kill us doesn't mean they don't make us want to do die. Just because they are benign doesn't mean they can brush us off and tell us to "just live it with" because what we have when they get bad isn't a life, it's merely and existence, and one that we probably wish would end. I know I did. I can't stand how powerless I feel. Every day the thought crosses my mind that I need to start a fundraiser for a cure or at least an awareness campaign, I need to write an article or something and find a way for it to get some attention, but I don't even know where to start. We should all be much more visible than we are.

LV: For me one of the hardest things is to try to explain how I feel and people get tired of listening and the fear once it takes hold just makes things worse. I read or clean the house or get out to be among friends. I figure if something were to happen I would rather be with people them alone.

DP: My story is slightly different to most in the fact that I don't have a structurally normal heart. Back in the late 90s I was 35 and had just had my 4th child. I felt continually exhausted, had begun to have palpitations and periods of dizziness. I had a difficult pregnancy and had been unwell with my gallbladder so put my symptoms down to that. The palpitations continued, I would get surges of what felt like adrenalin and I would sweat profusely. I went several times to my GP and to the A&E department to be told over and over again that it was anxiety. These episodes carried on for some years, and despite me having ECGS which showed Right Bundle Branch Block, (I was told it was sometimes a normal finding) I was never given an Echocardiogram. The diagnosis was always the same... (Anxiety!) Fast forward to 2013... I had just passed my 50th birthday. I was still suffering regular palpitations and what I believed to be 'panic attacks' but I also began to feel exhausted in a way which was difficult to explain. I felt as though I was walking through mud. My Mother had just passed away and I tried to put it down to grief but I had a nagging feeling something was very wrong. One night I was woken in the early hours by palpitations, sweating and what I believed to be panic yet again and when it wouldn't subside I decided to ring the emergency services. An ambulance was sent out and I was taken into the Hospital. For the first time ever, I was given an 'Echo' and it showed I had a very large Atrial Septal Defect between the two top chambers of my heart. I was told this would was 'Congenital' and would have been there since birth. Because I had lived so long with the defect I was suffering heart failure. The right side of my heart had enlarged and I had right mitral valve regurgitation. Other investigations went on to show I had mild pulmonary hypertension and was suffering atrial fibrillation and flutter. I had to have ablation treatment and isolation of the pulmonary vein. I eventually had the defect (hole) closed up with a device 12 months later in 2014. I still suffer palpitations and have to take high doses of propranolol. I also have Warfarin. I know this isn't exactly the same as some of your experiences but I can completely empathise when it comes to the anxiety these palpitations cause and how any problem with the heart can cause chronic health anxiety. I think for me the anxiety comes from the fact that so many years went by where my symptoms weren't taken seriously so now I always fear the worst. I will always have these palpitations because the structure of my heart will never be normal. It has totally changed my life. I find exercise difficult, I have little confidence, I don't go out anymore... if I do, it's never alone and I constantly fear the worst. I have lost a lot of confidence in the Health Service as a result which makes my health anxiety even worse. Any problem with the heart is debilitating and life changing. My heart (with its device!) goes out to you all and I hope you all get your problems treated successfully. Xxx

EA: I've thought about applying for disability pay because that's really what they are. They take so much out of me that I had my best friend in the world, my cat Brownie, certified as my emotional support pet. He has a kidney disease so sometimes we just lay in bed and be sick buddies, I don't know where I'd be without him. The thought of living with them for another 70 years is terrifying, but I would've though the same about 3 years when I was 17 and here I am, three years later and in a much better mental state than I was then. I can't thank you enough for creating this group, I know I'm not the only ones whose life has been saved because of it, and the lives we do live are that much easier to find fulfilment and strength in

AM: I have a few health issues, and my panic disorder plays a part in them all. My heart palpitations are my worst "condition", mentally speaking. Despite years of tests, therapy and medication, I cannot sever the primal connection in my brain that my heart is not beating properly therefore I am in danger. I can rationally tell myself a million times over I am ok. However, my body still has that hair trigger reaction of panic with each and every ectopic. Everything I do is with my heart in mind. I can't blame my agoraphobic behaviours solely on my palps but they are by far the strongest cause of fear and avoidance. My family and friends have come to accept I just can't do things. I have isolated myself to a bubble of false security. As sad and lonely as that feels, it beats the panic attacks that come with socializing and activity. I'm pretty hard on myself, I think we all are. I feel I am reasonably smart, and the fact I haven't been able to conquer these issues has me constantly questioning my intelligence. I admire and envy those with frequent ectopics that have been able to break the adrenaline surge and the mental/emotional effects of it, that they can live their lives despite their hearts beating out of rhythm.

NW: I ended up with PTSD and suspect that along with the high stress job I used to have for several years caused my palpitations which I've now had for 13 years. I had all of the tests and the structure is fine. However, many times I've been treated as if it's only "anxiety" and told not to worry (these people clearly never suffered with either palpitations or anxiety because "don't worry" doesn't work)

I can quite honestly say they have shrunken my world. I always wanted to travel now struggle to get out of my house some days and most days even out of my local area. I know that they won't kill you. However, when they occur logic goes out of the window as the autonomic system kick in and total anxiety ensues even before thoughts have a chance to start it. I always used to never understand why was meant by the feeling of impending doom felt by cardiac patients, now I really do it's instantaneous. So, whilst these may not affect my quantity of life, they have totally affected my quality of life.

TW: My palpitations started in 1999 when I was 23 and it completely shattered my world. It destroyed my sense of security and crushed my joy. I would lay in bed or sit on the sofa completely afraid to move for fear of causing my heart to go funny. I had the usual test - ekg, Holter, echo etc. The conclusion was I had benign ectopics. "Don't worry", said the Drs, "they're harmless". I should have been happy about that but I still felt terrified. There was no attainable information then. No Dr. Gupta YouTube videos, no Facebook support groups, no RLR. So, I trudged along and eventually became less afraid though not totally unafraid. Since then, I have had years where I lived my life relatively normally. I was able to work and travel and eat what I want. However, there have been many other times where the palpitations have filled me with such fear that I have been unable to work, unable to be social, unable to travel. I have been going through such a time since January where I am completely gripped by fear and anxiety about my palpitations. They're always in the back of my mind and the anxiety is a constant, unwelcome companion. It has impacted my life in every way. It is mentally and emotionally draining to be so anxious all the time. Every part of my life revolves around the palpitations. I'm afraid to eat certain foods for fear of causing them. I'm afraid to be too full because it makes me panicky. I'm afraid to bend over at times, afraid to do things to physically demanding. It is so tiring being in my head all of the time. To combat my fears, I am doing cognitive behavioural therapy and I also take anti-anxiety medication. I am doing better since January but I wish I was doing much better. Hopefully, I can conquer this fear once and for all because I can't imagine feeling this way for the rest of my life. My ectopics may be benign but the emotional, mental toll they have had on my life has been anything but benign.

TP: My palpitations started at age of 25 after having a bad infection. One evening I went into bigeminy and had SVT episode as well. I'm pretty sure the infection had something to do with it. Since then I've had pvcs every day for the last 4 years. I also get runs of pvcs(NSVT), PACs and SVT. Doctors did not believe me in the next day and said you are young, you cant have heart problems. It took a long time to get my arrhythmias on ECG. My SVT has become less frequent during these 4 years but the PVCs gets worse and worse every year. I have lots of stress because of these things and I don´t feel healthy. I struggle to keep my job, I can´t enjoy exercising anymore because of arrhythmias (I used to be a wrestler and train every day), I sold my kayak. I don´t enjoy travelling anymore because of the stress of having arrhythmias in a strange country and if I get a stomach bug I'm in a big trouble. So, I have given up these things pretty much; exercising, travelling, hiking, boating, coffee, alcohol, weed, running, wrestling, sauna, long rides with my motorcycle, partying and dancing. Pretty much everything exiting. Now I do what old people do; slow walks in the park, taking all kinds of pills, watching tv and writing here I'm so thankful about my GF, family and dog. They bring the most happiness in my life (sounds cheesy, I know

DE: Hiii !! I'm French and I'm 19 Yo and I live with my PVC and PAC since 2 years and I'm like you , I mean I have try to kill myself because I can't accept pvc and can't live with this shit and I'm too young to have heart problem, i have make a big depression and im fell really bad and today I have pvc every day of my life but I want destroy my palpitation I really want kill this shit because it's really hard to live with that when you are young like us ! I'm sorry for my English but you are like me and in same situation and we have to delete our problems of our heart and we have to LIIIIIVE like other young people so I'm with you and if you want you can add me to speak! Have a nice day and take care of you!! I have failed my suicide so now I don't want fail my fight against my heart!

As you will have read, the loss, the fear, the devastation to life is enormous. These are only a few voices of the seven thousand members of our Facebook group. The message is clear: telling people not to worry does not help. If statements like this did help, those who make them would be mighty rich to have conceived such a simple solution.

What I believe we need is hope. Hope can only come from the idea that there is movement in the medical community, in the form of research and understanding.

The following, full stories were gratefully received.

My Story by Emily Anne Albers

My story begins when I was a chubby, brace-faced, thirteen-year-old. I began to notice strange sensations in my heart from time to time, like it would momentarily forget how to beat. I didn't really think much of it, but I decided to get it checked out by a doctor anyway. At first, they didn't have a clue what was wrong with me, as my heart sounded normal when they listened to it. I had test after test done, and a few months later, after wearing a Holter monitor, I was diagnosed with PVCs. They told me there wasn't anything they could do for me, and at the time, I was satisfied in just knowing what they were. The PVCs were unpleasant, but they were rare and I was able to have a normal childhood, albeit with a few bothersome beats every few months or so. I managed to get through four years with relative ease. Then everything; my youthful life, my happiness, basically my ability to function all came to a screeching halt in my junior year of high school.

My hell began while I was already in hell, also known as school. I was sitting in class and I suddenly started having severe PVCs that wouldn't stop. I tried my best to get through the day, putting on my practiced calm face, while internally I was panicking. I'd never felt such an awful sensation in my life, I don't think there is anything that could ever compare. To my absolute dismay, they carried on into the night. This had never happened before, they had always gone away after a while.

My mom took me to the ER and by this point I was clutching my heart, shaking, sobbing uncontrollably, and could barely walk. Even though the doctors could clearly see the irregularity of the peaks and crests on the heart monitor and my grimace each time my heart fluttered, they told me it was nothing. They looked me in my eyes, irritated from the excessive crying, and told me that my PVCs may never stop, but I was fine and no treatment was needed for them. One doctor even had the audacity to laugh and reprimand me when my mom told him that they controlled every aspect of my life. He said, "Oh, she'll just have to learn to live with them" with a nonchalance that can only be found in someone who has never felt their heart, the organ keeping them alive, flopping and thudding and seizing every second of every day. I told him that suffering like this for the rest of my life wasn't an option. He told me to see a psychiatrist if I couldn't "cope" and handed us the discharge papers.

I was seventeen the night I came home from the ER. I'm twenty now, and the last three years have been spent trying to convince every cardiologist I could find that my PVCs were ruining not just my life, but hundreds of thousands of other compassionate, brave, undeserving people. Also, not only was treatment extremely necessary, but so was recognizing PVCs as a debilitating illness and making research a priority.
I even went as far as attempting suicide, not with the intention of killing myself, although my PVCs made me very tempted, but in the hopes of getting somebody, somewhere, to see that this "benign" condition that I shouldn't worry about because it won't kill me, was making me want to take my own life just to end the suffering.

Of course, they glossed over everything I said about my PVCs and came to the conclusion that I must just be mentally unstable, after all, PVCs are just a small nuisance, not enough to warrant such behavior. But the only thing that would fix my mind would be if something fixed my heart, so while the therapy did help with other unrelated aspects, it did nothing for the PVCs.

I did everything I possibly could to try and find a cure - biofeedback, meditation, seeing a chiropractor, vitamins, supplements, anti-anxiety meds, antidepressants, beta blockers, medical marijuana, diets, praying - and the only thing that ever came of it was getting my hopes up and then dashed into the ground over and over again, until I was so broken and hopeless I just gave up.

Begging and pleading with doctors to look into researching a cure, and when that failed, going on my own crusade to find one was my full-time job. When I had free time from it, I spent it lying in bed sobbing and clutching my heart, sick with rage and despair and loneliness and hopelessness.

Eventually that all faded into a gnawing emptiness, where I felt nothing but the horrendous thudding of my heart sputtering out of control. Sleep was difficult, but when it did come, it offered no respite, as I could feel my PVCs in my dreams. There was truly no escaping my own body. The only people who could help me feel better had dismissed or downplayed me, and my only solace was knowing I wasn't alone, that there were many, far too many people, who were going through the exact same thing.

This is what kept me going, and when my PVCs finally subsided after a few months and I could take my life off pause, I realized that even though I felt good, my life would never be the way it was before my PVCs had gotten worse. I had to give up so much of what I loved - caffeine, sugar, competitive swimming, talking for hours on end, my first job, moving away to go to college, the list goes on. But humans are an incredible species, we can adapt to whatever adversities life throws at us, and my PVCs became easier to manage each day. I stopped trying to fight them and ignore them, because the more I pretended I could live a normal life with them tormenting me, the more depressed I became. I tried to smile and laugh like everyone around me, but I was living in my own invisible hell. I was aware every second of the horrible sensations in my heart, and as long as I was feeling them, the only happiness I could ever have was feigned and hollow, a feeble attempt at what real happiness was supposed to be.

Contrary to the doctor's belief, there is no "living" with PVCs when I'm having them, I'm just existing and wishing that existence would end. So, I did what I tried to get the doctors to do for so long: I accepted my PVCs as a debilitating chronic illness and I treated them as such. I stayed in bed and rested when I wasn't feeling well, whether that was three days or three months. I'm not wasting my life, to me that would be trying to pretend that I'm healthy and happy when I'm not.

That's living a lie, and I'd rather lay in bed and feel terrible if that's the truth. When I feel better, I live my life to fullest and make up for the time I've lost and then some. Like grief, everyone has their own way of dealing with it, and this is what works for me in dealing with my PVCs. They have a mind of their own and can come out of nowhere with no rhyme or reason, so I never know when I wake up in the morning if this is my last day of joy and normalcy for a very long time.

Some can carry on with life while they have them, and others can't. For those who can't, for those who have exhausted every possible avenue and have nowhere else to turn but to the people who see our condition as nothing more than a minor inconvenience, I have this to say: don't lose hope. If you're unable to live with your suffering, you have to know that you're not crazy, you're not at fault, you're not weak, you're not less than because you can't overcome an impossible obstacle.

No matter what anyone says, we know the only solution for us is a cure, and we will stop at nothing until we find it. We're all in this together, we've been there for each other with support and understanding when no one else was, and if we all can raise our voices and tell our stories and make not just our suffering, but our passion and desperation for a cure known to everyone in the medical field and beyond, then one day we could live in the world we've always dreamed of - one without PVCs.

My Story by Kathy Jordan

It was Christmas Eve 1984 when my palpitations began. I was 21 years old, slender, very active, a non-smoker and I never drank alcohol or used drugs. By all accounts I was healthy. The only thing I can think of that could have triggered them, is long term high stress levels.

The palpitations quickly became more frequent and I spoke with my family doctor. He dismissed it as nerves and suggested I just ignore them. This is much easier said than done. I ended up back in his office sooner than expected. He finally sent me for a work up by a cardiologist. I had all the usual tests, echocardiogram, ekg and holter monitors galore. Test results showed premature atrial and ventricle contractions and some svt. I was started on a beta blocker, which relieved some of my symptoms, but still some days it was very hard to concentrate on doing every day, simple tasks. As the years passed I saw numerous doctors and had repeated tests. The side effects of the beta blockers took a toll. Fatigue, weight gain, thinning hair, enlarged atrium and ventricle, swelling and shortness of breath were difficult to deal with as well as the ectopics.

As time went on, the palpitations continued to worsen. Still, I tried very hard to live my life as the doctors would encourage. I managed to marry, start a family and a career. I wish I could say they were a success, but the truth is, all suffered greatly from my everyday struggles with this issue. I couldn't plan any activity because there were days I couldn't function at all. The eptopics were so frequent I was ill on the sofa or in bed. I missed a great deal of work due to being unable to function and eventually lost jobs. I could not think clearly on the days the palpitations were very frequent and I would become very faint and, on several occasions, I did suffer syncope. I finally had to resign the last position I held in the special education field. My marriage failed from the stresses of my being ill so much of the time. I became quite agoraphobic. My son struggled terribly with having a Mother too sick to do things like other parents, which gave him a heightened fear of death and losing his Mom. To this day as an adult I can still see the scars he has from it. So many everyday things most people take for granted aren't easy for those of us that live with arrhythmias.

My anxiety was intense and I was always conscious of how I sat, bent over and what I could pick up, without causing my heart to go out of rhythm. I'm always cautious of what I eat or drink because so many foods and additives cause me terrible palpitations, as well as the amount I can intake. I could not travel or drive alone. When I do manage to go out, I am always aware of where the exits are located and sit near them in case I go into an abnormal rhythm.

I noticed a difference in my palpitations around 2001. I repeated all the tests and had multiple Holter monitors. I requested a long term 60-day monitor and it showed I was having short bursts of atrial fibrillation. Since then my episodes of afib have become more frequent and longer.

More meds, more side effects. In 2017 I had a loop recorder implanted hoping to get a clearer picture of what was happening so that my treatment could be adjusted to better control my symptoms, because that is all we are doing, being as no one can pinpoint a cause. The loop recorder has shown some atrial tachycardia along with the afib, pvcs and pacs. I have been told by my electrophysiologist that some readings are still of an undetermined nature. I know there is some debate whether palpitations can transform into something more dangerous; as far as I'm concerned, for me at least, the answer is a definite yes.

My symptoms during my more severe arrhythmia episodes are quite unnerving. At the onset I immediately know it's different than my every day, all day pvcs and pacs. I become short of breath almost immediately as my heart races upward toward the 200 bpm. I then get erratic beats in the sequence as I try to stay clear minded as possible in case it doesn't subside and I need to ask for help. I check to see if there is anyone nearby and it's second nature to check for my phone and now to grab my Loop Recorder Wand. As the seconds pass I begin to tremble all over and thinking becomes more difficult. After approximately a minute, tunnel vision sets in and I become extremely weak. At this point breathing is laboured in the same way as when I experience atrial fibrillation with Rapid Ventricle Response (RVR).

After these episodes I experience a period of time when my heart, my nerves and my anxiety is hypersensitive. Driving is extremely difficult all the time because of the fear of causing an accident or killing someone or myself.

I am very sensitive to vibrations and loud noises and have been for many years. Concerts, loud vehicles, motorcycles, sitting on a riding lawn mower, standing on a surface where machinery such as a pressure washer in use, etc. Even driving on some highways that have grooves placed in a particular pattern, will cause me heart irregularities and I will have to immediately remove myself from that area or exit the highway before it gets worse.

I have noticed that due to the ongoing stress with my heart all of the time has meant my immune system has taken a beating and does not seem to function properly. I am always fighting off some kind of virus or illness. Stress caused by fear of death, anxiety, sadness, depression, agoraphobia, all a huge part of this monster we live with daily. This is an illness that I believe has not been given enough attention. There are many facets to it and it will steal your life as well as those around you. There is always a dark cloud over me. I know that if I'm having a good day that the worst is right around the corner.

The Magnitude of these symptoms cannot be explained here in words. My desire is that there will be many more studies devoted to get a better understanding of arrhythmias, their causes and treatments.

We desperately need better care and support systems in place for those of us who suffer daily with this illness. I am very grateful to be given this opportunity to tell my story and maybe reading this will give someone else a sense of hope and let them know they are not alone.

My story by L. MacDiarmid

I remember being 9 years old and feeling a strange fluttering sensation in my throat from time to time but being young I never thought anything of it and certainly didn't think it was anything to do with my heart. They were so few and far between that they never bothered me at all. I grew up, left home for University, partied hard, lived a full and fun filled life without a care in the world. Again, the occasional flutter, but it didn't really bother me.

Fast forward to turning 30. Life was good, I had finished a shift as Staff Nurse in ITU and was walking home when suddenly I felt a huge thump right in my chest, this was followed by another and another and another. Instinctively, I felt my pulse and noticed there was a pause which correlated with the thuds. Panicked, I called my husband who came and picked me up. By the time he arrived, it had stopped and I had calmed down. I saw my GP who ordered the usual tests. Sure enough, the Holter monitor came back as picking up ectopic beats. I was sent on my merry way and told they were benign and to just get on with my life which I did.

They didn't bother me again for another 4 years until I became pregnant with my eldest son. My pregnancy was stressful as our boy was diagnosed with Spina Bifida, Hydrocephalus and other associated medical conditions. The ectopics were constant whilst I was pregnant and continued after he was born. They became unbearable and when my son was around 1, I completely broke down. The anxiety they caused was unbelievable, I felt trapped in my own body; I couldn't escape the funky beats, they were constant and I became terrified that I was going to die and leave my baby motherless. It got so bad that I wrote a book about everything my husband needed for our son, his routines, favourite toys, favourite way to sleep etc, it was such a dark, dark time and the doctors just kept saying I was depressed and not listening to me about my concerns about my heart. It took a long time and lots of effort but, by changing my diet, making time for rest and exercise, they became bearable and less frequent and life became fun again.

I felt so much better until I fell pregnant with another baby boy. The palpitations were fine until I delivered my son and the same thing happened again, they became relentless, they really broke me and I'd never felt so low in my entire life. It was so hard dealing with a child with additional needs, a tiny refluxy baby and a husband who worked a stressful job, 14 hours a day and was never home. I've never felt so desperate. Again, doctors just told me they were benign and not to worry, but the anxiety these beats caused constantly was unbearable. Again, I worked really hard with my diet, exercise, rest and antidepressants along with CBT and a psychologist. I'm back living my life again but it's a different life. I've lost a lot of confidence, career and friends. I rarely socialise outside my comfort circle, mainly family and close friends, but I'm doing the things I need to do, my kids don't miss out and I'm back traveling abroad again, something I thought I'd never do!

I still get them all the time but I'm not as in tune to them as I used to be. When I think about how desperate I was 8 years ago and how far I've come, I almost can't believe it's the same person. Don't get me wrong I still have a wobble now and then if they increase in volume but I'm ALMOST used the funky way my heart beats now. It's a part of me, it's not going to go away, it hasn't killed me yet and I don't intend to waste any more years putting my life on hold! I'm seizing the day now and clawing back the life I've lost.

My Story by H.R

My (noticeable) heart palpitations began the day after the birth of my daughter, seventeen years ago. I'd developed pre-eclampsia which had become so severe, an emergency C-Section had to be performed, two months before my daughter's due date at St George's in Tooting, South London.

One of the prep procedures they performed was inserting a wire through a main artery and into my heart. I have no idea as to the exact technicalities of this procedure though I was told it was to control my heart rate and prevent a heart attack.

After the operation, the wire should have been instantly removed, but it was forgotten. It was only when I complained to a nurse some days after the operation that my heart was "fluttering" that the wire was removed and I was placed on beta blockers.

The palpitations eventually went away and I forgot all about them – I never even gave them a second thought to be honest. Five years later, shortly after the 7/7 attacks here in London, I was on a tube train with my daughter when we were evacuated due to a bomb alert. Having lived in London since I was a teenager, I am well used to bomb alerts and indeed, I have been in the close proximity of several IRA bombs during the 1980's and 1990's however, on this particular occasion, I was petrified. I became overwhelmed with fear and ended up having a full-blown panic attack which was so severe, I physically couldn't get back on to the tube.

From this singular panic attack, I developed severe anxiety disorder and with that came some very scary heart palpitations. Flutters, huge bangs in my chest, heart racing and eventually "runs" of palpitations which were utterly terrifying. So terrifying that I felt sure I would die. I would be struck with severe dizziness and felt like I physically couldn't pull any air into my lungs.

I want to say here that my life has not been an easy one – it has been stressful from a very young age. I was abandoned by my father (I eventually met him for the very first time a few years ago), sexually abused and raped by my first step-father when I was a child. I lived with a mother who suffered with severe depression and occasional dark, dark moods which I had to learn to manage. I was for a time fostered by my aunt and uncle (in Virginia where I grew up) and went to many schools, always learning to cope with being the "new girl". At 17, my mother left me, so I moved to London and worked very hard to support myself. I come from the kind of family where a "stiff upper lip" is mandatory. We are not allowed to feel sorry for ourselves, complain or ask for help. Therefore, I had nobody to help me and I learned, from a young age, how to cope with stress. I mention all of this because I want to make it clear that extreme stress has been part and parcel of my life – I am well used to coping with it and I have faced some truly terrifying experiences. It could be possible that, on that particular day on the Central line, my stress levels finally caused my system to crash but whatever the cause, I have since had to learn to live with heart palpitations and all they bring with them.

I have had numerous ECG's; chest x-rays, blood tests and even a heart scan – all perfectly normal. Does this comfort me? Yes, to an extent. However, it is of no comfort whatsoever when these things strike, particularly when out in public or trapped in a car or on public transport. If they can strike fear into me, they can strike fear into anyone.

They have absolutely taken away a certain peace of mind and fearlessness that I once enjoyed and took for granted. However, the fighter inside of me refuses to let them take more than they deserve and actually, I have learned to see them instead as a "gift". Because of my heart palpitations, I took a diploma in Nutrition and learned to live a healthier life. I have studied stress-management, learned Yoga, learned to meditate, learned breathing techniques and through my experience and knowledge, have been able to help others. I count myself very lucky indeed that my heart is structurally fine – I know many others are not so fortunate and suffer greatly with some rather serious health concerns.

Some things I've found which help me are eating avocados, eggs and taking liquid iron (sachets) in addition to taking folic acid, eating a healthy balanced diet overall and drinking lots of water. Walking is a daily part of my life along with weekly weight bearing exercises which I find help to keep my stress levels in check and use up lots of nervous energy. Getting a decent night of sleep is also very important – if I don't have a good night of sleep then I can guarantee I will get some heart skips and flutters the following day.

Two years ago, I lost my mother to early on-set dementia. This was a very stressful eight-year period from which I emerged finally understanding that life is indeed extremely short and should never be taken for granted. If I suddenly keel over from these wretched things, so be it – after all, I'm going to keel over at some point. In the meantime, I'm not going to waste any further time worrying about them. I've learned to accept and live with them because I have no other choice. I've been to rock concerts with 20,000 other people, I've been in the middle of the forest with not another soul around – I don't let them stop me from living the life that I deserve to have and I would wish for others exactly the same.

My Story by G.S

I first experienced palpitations aged 49, when I first missed a period and I started the phase of life known as peri-menopause. Whenever I skipped a monthly bleed, two days before the next one happened I had up to 36 hours of bigeminy (every other beat is an ectopic beat). This totally terrified me and took a while for me to notice the pattern. I was eventually referred to a cardiologist who dismissed any hormonal link but confirmed frequent PVCs and put me on bisoprolol – a beta blocker. For me, as for many women going through a similar phase this just made me very tired and made my palpitations come on daily. After about six months I gave up on it and tried a couple of other medications which the cardiologist suggested but which didn't suit me. The reassurance from the cardiologist that these were harmless 'heart hiccups' was really important and helped me keep calmer when the skipped beats were happening. I found that drinking a cup of either chamomile or mistletoe tea was very helpful to reduce the palpitations as was keeping well hydrated. I think I tried every supplement and alternative therapy going in an attempt to find an answer as to why I was having these things! Nothing seemed to really work.

As time went on and my bleeds became much further apart the palpitations occurred more frequently due to the random hormone fluctuations that can be experienced at this time. I also developed reactive hypoglycaemia, which also causes me to have palpitations when my blood sugar drops. This was controlled by eating every 2-3 hours. I basically split a normal meal into two and eat half as a meal and half as a snack to make sure I do not increase my calorie intake. As part of the diagnosis of the reactive hypoglycaemia I was referred to an endocrinologist who referred me onto a different cardiologist to look at the increased irregular heartbeats. This time I was diagnosed as having short runs of SVT as well as the frequent PVCs. This cardiologist totally acknowledged the link between hormonal fluctuations and an irregular heart rhythm – in fact I was the fourth lady of a similar age he had seen that day with the same symptoms. This was a huge relief to me and he was very reassuring saying that although this can go on for several years it would eventual settle down as the hormones settle down. After using Flecainide as a 'pill-in-the-pocket' for a year he decided that I should go on a low dose daily as I was still having very frequent bouts of bigeminy and trigeminy. Within three days the palpitations completely stopped. I am 57 now and the cardiologist hopes that in a few years I will be able to stop taking the Flecainide. Whilst I was originally apprehensive about taking a daily medication as I prefer to treat myself naturally where possible I have to admit that the Flecainide has given me back a quality of life that I thought I had lost. It has made an amazing difference to me to be free of these funky beats after eight years.

My Story by Jen Penrose

Looking back, I think I began experiencing ectopic heart beats around 2005. At that time, I experienced what felt like a pulse in my stomach. This feeling would happen mostly after eating in the evening. I later discovered this pulse feeling would also happened each time I attempted to give up cigarettes using nicotine patches. The pulsating feeling was rare and never bothered me. Possibly because I had no idea it was my heart and therefore not being fearful may have played a big part in things not worsening at that time.

In 2007, aged 57, I moved from a small house to a slightly larger one where we began work on an extension. Anyone who has experience of living in building site conditions, might understand the amount of stress I was under. In 2008, while everything was still in a mess and with lots of interior work going on, I decided for the umpteenth time to stop smoking again; once again using nicotine patches. The stomach pulsating started up again, only this time it was stronger. I also started to suffer from acid reflux, which I now believe was a sensitivity to the patches, or perhaps it was the stress of the building work, or both.

I reported the symptoms to my GP who referred me for a 24 Holter Monitor (24-hour ECG) which showed runs of ectopic beats of the atria (PAC's) with some running up to 18 consecutive beats. I continued giving up the cigarettes and using the patches, not linking the physical symptoms to them, or the stress.

I had an office in my home and worked from there two and a half days of the week. This in itself was difficult because any interior work to the house was delayed by lack of access. Feeling down and stressed, the symptoms became worse and worse, in particular the acid reflux. I developed oesophageal spasms and anyone who has experienced those will know the chest pain is unbearable and can mimic heart attack.

In late 2008, I came down from upstairs and entered my office. I was stressed and edgy. As I entered the room I blacked out momentarily. I found myself on the floor feeling slightly dazed but intact. I put it down to rushing. The pulsations in my stomach continued but not often and I chose to ignore them.

In early 2009, on arising one morning, with my 24-hour nicotine patch on and a throat full of acid, I began to cough and my heart took off and it felt as though it would beat its way right out of my chest. My husband called an ambulance who took me to A and E. Some of the time I was in normal sinus rhythm (NSR) and some of the time my heart rate was really fast and I felt faint. The feeling was scary and I thought my time was up.

In hospital, things began to calm down and I was sent home with a beta blocker. Approximately an hour after taking it, I began to wheeze badly. I called my surgery and a GP I spoke to, told me not to take any more. I am lucky enough to have a good GP, who does what he can to help me, within the bounds of his medical protocols and ethics.

From that day on, I experienced many PAC's and PVC's, all day every day. There were days where just walking from one room to the other felt impossible – I was sure I would die, despite being reassured I would not.

This situation went on for many years. For two of those, I hardly went out and when I did I had to be accompanied. Even with someone else with me it was not unknown for me to turn back. I had no social life other than a small group of counsellors whom I met with once per month, in relation to counselling workshops we ran four times a year. I remember hanging on to the side of my chair throughout workshops, and I would insist on sitting near to the door. Health anxiety, medication anxiety, agoraphobia and claustrophobia invaded my days. I think the most painful thing was how I felt about myself. It is not an exaggeration to say I felt a lesser person.

My belief is that people who do not suffer from, or fully understand anxiety, will sometimes condemn it. We seem to be currently living in a culture of negative judgement over poor physical and mental health. It is quite the thing to say I am fine, even if the person's leg is hanging off by a thread of skin!
Brave and strong are modern buzz words. Perhaps this is a humorous take on it, but from my experience, people will defend against ill health in the same way they defend against death anxiety; it happens to other people. Worse, anxiety, I think, is often viewed as a weakness.

There were people who spoke to me or treated me as though I'd lost my intellect; that anything I had to say was from a place of weakness and therefore cannot hold much weight. Of course, I felt this way about myself too. This caused me to spiral down, hating the idea of needing other people, and yet being a grateful victim of their help.

When I found the forum 'No More Panic' (1), things began to change. I no longer felt isolated with the condition and had somewhere to talk with people without feeling judged. It was very uplifting for me. Then later, when I signed up to Dr. Rane's forum (3) and read his answers to members questions, I started to recover a little. It never ceases to amaze me how empathy can be so healing.

I began to force myself to go for short walks alone. Then longer walks. I went to the cinema with trusted people and began socialising generally. At first it took everything I had to overcome the fear, but eventually, after about a year of working hard to recover my life, I was starting to live again.

However, the palps still made their presence known, although they were less because I was not feeding them with more fear and stress. During this time, I realised the cause of my heart turbulence was in relation to two things: Stress and GERD. I think the first brought about the latter.

More recently I was hospitalised with two, separate attacks of AF. Both episodes were initiated by severe bouts of GERD. All the strength I had built up over the years was destroyed and replaced by an awful doomsday feeling, along with overwhelming panic attacks.

The acid, I believe, penetrated that 5mm of tissue between the left atrium and the oesophagus mentioned earlier, causing inflammation to the vagus nerve. This means I am currently suffering horrendous palps, and short but disabling afib attacks. I dread the next full on attack and have become obsessed with keeping my stomach acid at bay.

My social life consists of hospital visits. I have two good friends who will ferry me to and from appointments when I need them too – but our interaction mostly ends there. We may chat on those days – but I am unable to organise anything else; never knowing what my heart has planned for me.

I think a huge percent of people will have a similar story. Many like me will struggle to keep hoping that one day we will be free. I think that will only happen if more research takes place. It cannot happen without recognition of the ongoing trauma and devastation we all suffer.

Addendum

Being at the editing stage of this book, I thought it might be a good idea to check if anyone else had written a book about palpitations. I searched Amazon first of all, typing in the word palpitations. There were a few fiction books with the word palpitation in the title and one self-help ebook by Nick Walsh and Morgan Adams called – How to Stop or Prevent Heart Palpitations, 2013, (25). The book appears to be written solely by Nick Walsh and although the title is advertised as above, the book title on the front cover reads differently as: 7 Proven Methods to Prevent Heart Palpitations. This might mean that a new cover was uploaded sometime after the book was published.

Nick writes in relation to his own palpitations and a couple of episodes of AF. He describes the losses and stresses he endured leading up to the episodes. He takes a similar view to me because he feels doctors in general, seem uninterested in the cause. His view is from the perspective of an American based medical system, and therefore money for medical care is a big part of his conversation. He speaks of big Pharma companies that he believes own the doctors. What I can relate to is the idea that drugs are big business and research is generally undertaken by Pharma companies. Alternative and natural medicines and home remedies are very under-researched and not offered as medical treatment. We do not have holistic practitioners within our medical systems. Imagine clinics full of alternative practitioners where your whole body and mind was being thought about and treated.

Darian Leader and David Corfield in their book: Why Do People Get Ill, 2007, write that: "Payment methods in insurance-based systems tend to reward costly technical procedures, not listening processes. In some parts of America, a physician will only get reimbursed for a consultation if it results in a prescription. The power of drug companies has likewise grown exponentially. They now fund about two thirds of clinical studies, and medical journals have increasingly become marketing devices for new products and diagnoses. After thirteen years editing the British Medical Journal, Richard Smith concluded that the studies funded by industry are subtly manipulated to give positive results." (26)

They go on to state:

"The expansion of alternative practices is sometimes explained as a consequence of the medical professions unwillingness to listen to its patients. For much of the medicine practiced today, the body is merely the sum of its parts and little more."

Nick Walsh (25), like myself, believes that inflammation is the root cause of illness. He offers plenty of ideas on how to keep inflammation at bay and shares his own regime, which he says has cured him. Feeling disappointed with medicine and doctors, he felt he had no choice but to research and develop his own, individual treatment. He believes, as do I, that doctors are less interested in cause and more interested in the symptom(s). He says:

"When was the last time any of your doctors actually sat you down and said, together…you and me…we're going to find out what is causing these palpitations and we are going to find the cure."

Interestingly, Nick lists very similar symptoms to my own and those of RS:

- Tightness in the throat
- Feeling of rapid pulse
- Dizziness
- Feeling faint
- Passing out
- Sweating
- High fear and anxiety
- Fear of exercising
- Fear of going out of the house

He goes on to say: "In most cases people that experience palpitations have a twofold problem. Not only are they genuinely suffering from palpitations, but they also suffer from what I call collateral anxiety disorder (CAD)."

What I think he means by collateral anxiety disorder, is that of the collateral damage many are left with. The fear, anxiety and phobias that we sufferers are dealing with, and in some cases reports on our Facebook page of being berated by their doctor and even shouted at for feeling frightened.

I would recommend the book mentioned above, by Darian Leader and David Corfield; Why Do People

Get Ill. I met Darian Leader when I was part of a counselling group of four who organised workshops for local counsellors. We invited Darian to come and speak to us about why people get ill, and his talk was fascinating. Equally, the book offers lots of information and is filled with great insights.

Conclusion

I had intended this book to be more of a pamphlet. Once I began writing I realised fairly quickly that there was so much to put forward. What felt most important to me was being able to connect with other sufferers of heart arrhythmia, with empathy and understanding. I had hoped to reassure in some way that you are not alone, because the condition is so very isolating and confusing. Knowing how hard it is to explain the condition to people and get understanding of how tired and fearful many of us feel, I wanted to produce something that sufferers would be able to relate to and hand to their medical practitioners, their families and their friends.

I have watched over the years, as members spill their pain, confusion, fear, loss and sadness on to our Facebook group page. I have witnessed members supporting each other, even when they themselves are suffering. They are all incredibly brave. You see, being brave is not being fearless, it is feeling frightened and carrying on regardless. Mothers and Fathers continue to care for their children, braving each day to do so. All of them continue to get up in the morning and try to proceed with courage and often with humour.

My wonderful friend Kathy who is an admin on our Facebook group and who submitted her story, pushes on each day, caring for her family, providing sanctuary for cats, continuing to help and support other members, even though she feels so very unwell most of the time. So brave, and so inspiring.

My thanks to Kathy, to H.R, L. MacDiarmid, Emily and G.S, who so bravely shared their stories in the hope that we may at last get recognition for our distress and that we may inspire more research. And my grateful thanks for the members who allowed me to publish their posts.

What I have written can and will create more questions: Is it saying treat your stomach and everything will be fine? Is the problem an exhausted and out of sync nervous system? Is it anxiety or stress? Is my endocrine system not functioning fully? And so on.

Interestingly, stress and electrolyte imbalance can create endocrine imbalances and endocrine imbalances will cause disruption of the body's fine tuning. As you will by now have gathered, I am suspicious that generally, heart palps, stomach acid, dizzy spells, hormone imbalances and even Roemheld Syndrome itself, unless relating to a known and specific cause, are symptoms of wider issues that I believe can only be exposed through investigation and research.

In the meantime, we can review our lifestyles; our diet, our stresses and how or if they can be removed, even if that means unfriending negative people, our exercise regime and how much relaxation we allocate ourselves. Most of all, do not accept the idea that we have to get on with it, at least not without exhausting all avenues to healing.

I am disappointed that I have not produced more of a self-help style of book. I would like so much to offer a solution. What I hope is that this book at the very least encourages further thinking with us, and with our doctors. I hope it sparks other ideas; ones that I have missed or have not researched as well as I might have.

We want medicine to think outside of the box; to be more innovative about this condition and accept that palpitations are not harmless; they cause anguish and loss and we want this to be acknowledged and supported. Growth comes from change, and change comes about through an openness to new ideas.

A long-term dream has been to have a manned helpline and/or information line. If this condition could be classified as a disability, I see no reason why a small charity could not be set up for support and for the funding of research.

I conclude by thanking you for reading my short, Facebook group inspired writings, and for being part of the palp journey with us.

Peace and love to you all.

Links and References:

1: Facebook Group – https:www.facebook.com/groups/heartpalps/

2: No More Panic – http://www.nomorepanic.co.uk

3: Rutheford Rane's Forum – http://chemicalforums.com/cgi-bin/YaBB.pl?board=general

4: Endocrine Disrupting Chemicles - https://www.hormone.org/hormones-and-health/endocrine-disrupting-chemicals

5: Human Hormones – BBC Bitesize http://www.bbc.co.uk/schools/gcsebitesize/science/aqua_pre_2011/human/hormonesrev1.shtml

6: Panic Attacks Free course – http://panic-attacks.co.uk/course/

7: Healthline – All about Electrolyte Disorders – https://healthline.com/health/electrolyte-disorders

8: Sanjay Gupta
- Website: http://yorkcardiology.com/
- YouTube channel: https://www.youtube.com/channel/UCxtbUzEzRpX1B9sGbRudG6g
- Facebook: https://www.facebook.com/yorkcardiology1/

9: Cure PVC's – www.curepvcs.com

10: Dive reflex by Steve Mensing – http://www.self-helpapedia.com/thedivereflex.htm

11. 'Om' Chanting – Ijoy International Journal of Yoga – http://www.ncbi.nlm.nih.gov/pmc/articles/PMC3099099/?report=printable

12: International Journal of Recent Trends in Science and Technology – Therapeutic effects of Music Listening: http://statperson.com/Journal/ScienceandTechnology/Article?SpecialIssue/ACAEE_14.pdf

13: Depression and Inflammation: https://www.ncbi.nlm.nih.gov/labs/articles/27337107/n

14: Depression and Inflammation: https://www.psychologytoday.com/us/blog/urban-survival/201701/new-research-shows-depression-lonked-inflammation

15: How Stress influences disease 2012 https://www.sciencedaily.com/releases/2012/04/120402162546.htm

16: Super Human Radio – Roemheld Syndrome https://app.box.com/s/aqlw20oafjkj289pyqac

17: Bad Wildungen- Lecture Breathing Exercises for Roemheld Syndrome – 1984 http://www.xn--dpmartinjunghfer-ywb.de/pdf/Breath%20Training%20for%20Roemheld%20Syndrome.pdf

18: World Journal of Gastroenterology 2014 - https://www.ncbi.nlm.nih.gov/pmc/articles/PMC4110594/

19: Deglutition-Induce Atrial Fibrillation -Texas Heart Institute Journal – 2015 https://www.ncbi.nlm.nih.gov/pmc/articles/PMC1351842/

20: Yoga U – Tapping into the Power of the Vagus Nerve https://www.yogauonline.com/yoga-for-stress-relief/tapping-power-vagus-nerve-how-your-breath-can-change-your-relationships

21: Yoga International – Soothe Your Nervous System –
https://yogainternational.com/article/view/soothe-your-nervous-system-with-2-to-1-breathing

22: Max Strom – Breath to Heal –
https:www.youtube.com/watch?v=4Lb5L-VEm34&t=126s&index=75&list=PLKG7bUsSdIH760QqKSIMPV63D2_eyADXW

23: The European Society of Cardiology 2017 –
https://academic.oup.com/eurospace/article

24: Robert A Ganz MD – Endoscopic Therapies for Gastroesophageal Reflux Disease
https://www.ncbi.nlm.nih.gov/pmc/articles/PMC4969778

25: Seven Proven Methods to Prevent Heart Palpitations 2013 – Nick Walsh and Morgan Adams

26: Why do People Get Ill - 2007   Darian Leader and David Corfield

Made in the USA
Monee, IL
22 April 2024

57306626R00066